THE FOUNDING

*A Memoir of the Early Years of
the Arvon Foundation*

THE FOUNDING OF ARVON

*A Memoir of the Early Years of
the Arvon Foundation*

JOHN MOAT

FRANCES LINCOLN

THE FOUNDING OF ARVON

Frances Lincoln Limited
4 Torriano Mews
Torriano Avenue
London NW5 2RZ
www.franceslincoln.com

Text copyright © 2005 John Moat

First Frances Lincoln edition: 2005

ISBN 10: 0-7112-2452-8
ISBN 13: 978-0-7112-2588-6

Printed and bound in Singapore
by KHL Printing Co Pte Ltd

2 4 6 8 9 7 5 3 1

Also by John Moat

POETRY

Thunder of Grass
6d per annum
Skeleton Key
Fiesta & Fox Reviews His Prophesy
The Welcombe Overtures
Firewater & the Miraculous Mandarin
Practice (with drawings)
The Valley (with drawings)
100 Poems
Hermes & Magdalen

NOVELS

Heorot
Bartonwood
Mai's Wedding
The Missing Moon

SHORT STORY
Rain

ALSO
The Standard of Verse

AND WITH JOHN FAIRFAX
The Way to Write

www.johnmoat.co.uk

CONTENTS

For the friends and the Friends of Arvon

All thanks to Sue Stewart for her guidance and editing, to Antoinette for an alternative memory, to Jane Lane for suggestions and crucial acerbities, and to Julia Wheadon who searched the attic. My thanks also to the Friends of Arvon and my special contact Mavis Carter for their support.

J.M.

When the Arvon student is put in possession of that creative self, which was hitherto inaccessible, two things, in particular, suddenly become much more interesting: the working of language, and the use of literature. In other words, that event brings about, often in a very short time, but in an organic and natural way, what years of orthodox English teaching almost inevitably fail to bring about, except in the most artificial and external way. The student is awakened to the real life of language, with all that implies of the physiology of words, their ancestry and history and dynamic behaviour in varying circumstances (of all abbreviated, in conventional teaching, under the heading: grammar). At the same time he is introduced to literature as a living organism, part of the human organism, something which embodies the psychological record of this drama of being alive, something which articulates and illuminates the depth and range and subtlety of being human. Literature becomes as personal to him as his own struggling abilities – no longer, as conventional teaching presents it (and can only present it), a museum of obsolete manners and dead artefacts, without any relevance to 'now and the future'.

And in all this, the student has not swallowed anything from outside. It has all been awakened inside. In the true sense of the word he has been 'educated'.

Ted Hughes, from his Foreword to
Fairfax's and Moat's *The Way to Write*

But yield who will to their separation,
My object in living is to unite
My avocation and my vocation
As my two eyes make one in sight.
Only where love and need are one,
And the work is play for mortal stakes,
Is the deed ever really done
For Heaven and the future's sakes.

Robert Frost, *Two Tramps in Mudtime*

BEHIND THE BEGINNING

After breakfast the first morning Fairfax and I lost our way. I doubt either of us could ever have told you what a seminar is. But suddenly 'the voices of our accursed education' were whispering that after Poet's Stew something more substantial, like a seminar, was needed to get us back on track. So that's what we convened, a seminar on the grass in the Centre's garden. We knew that a seminar was serious business, and that to qualify we couldn't get away with anything light-weight. Prosody!

We were five halting minutes into the subject of prosody when arrested by a groan indicative of severe bellyache. One of the Crediton Three had rolled on to his back and was glaring at the sky. 'I thought,' he muttered with menace, 'we were here to do writing.' This was 1968, don't forget – there was a whiff of cordite, hot from the barricades. Fairfax and I glanced at each other, and then nodded. 'You thought right,' we said. And that concluded the seminar. It was, in my judg-ment, the moment Arvon came into being.

So then the rest was history? Not exactly – not if one assumes the historical period must to some extent be verifi-able. If that's the case, Arvon's history begins some six years later. This book is about the prehistoric period and so alto-gether something different. Like what, fiction? Fairfax and I would raise a glass to that, though there would be some splut-tering over whose version of Arvon's prehistory should be The Authorised. Here's mine.

The private prep school in question is today a model of excellence. But at the time, the early 1960s, it was, as we would then have said, 'unreal'. Quite beyond fiction's reach, unless Evelyn Waugh's *Decline and Fall* could be relocated in

Mervyn Peake's *Gormenghast*. But where else would Fairfax, and then in due turn Moat, have found employment? If you can call it employment where the salary is part of the overall fiction. Still, for two young poets on the run from fiscal reality, it offered some sort of sanctuary. Unlike London, it offered a roof.

First came Fairfax – mid-twenties, well-thrashed by his attempts (cub reporter, private eye, Customs and Excise supernumerary, encyclopedia salesman, driving instructor . . .) to have his wife Esther, his son Michael, and his determination to write poems, survive together in London. An advertisement offering a roof was decisive. And if surety of a roof needed to involve teaching, then so be it. It's tempting to write more about the school but maybe it is enough to say that there were ways in which Fairfax was well suited. Clearly so because after a couple of years he was sufficiently revived to tilt at the world again. He discovered in a wood near by the old thatched gamekeeper's cottage, then derelict, that would be his, Esther's, Michael's, and by now Jonathan's home. The Thatched Cottage has cared for him ever since.

The legacy Fairfax left to the school was a situation vacant. And so by the same path of no option came this other in his mid-twenties, away from the same London, similarly thrashed mindless by the same ineffectual attempt to write poems and unlikely fiction and survive. A random coincidence? It has to be more likely that under cover the Arvon agency was already in operation. I had no idea in whose footsteps I served my two vacant years before the blackboard. Fairfax was mentioned occasionally, along with the suggestion 'You ought to meet him, you'd have something in common,' the tone of which didn't do either much credit. A poet, poems . . . in my state of health? No thanks.

It may be that life in the school was so far beneath the surface that being submerged in it (and, I tell you, engaged from 7.00 am to midnight, there was no coming up for air) worked like a therapeutic coma: one's sense of defeat in the real world could find in this context nothing to relate to, and so ceased to interfere with the natural process of healing. In my second year I began to write again. Each evening I'd steal an hour, drive to The Fox, set myself up in a corner of the quiet lounge bar with a pint, and write. This way, hour by hour, over a year I produced a new draft of my first novel – and that allowed me to feel maybe it was time to test my footing back in the real world once more.

So then one night I went for a drink in another pub – and got talking to this bloke with an ominous shine to him sat at the bar. At the end of the evening, because we hadn't finished our conversation, I went back to his place. Three in the morning and we still hadn't finished our conversation. That was Fairfax, and forty years later it seems we still haven't finished that conversation.

I'll tell you an odd thing. When Arvon had been going for twenty-five years the then Chairman, Lawrence Sail, out of the particular generosity of his, organised a surprise lunch party for the founders in this good country restaurant. We were into the pudding when Fairfax pointed to where, twelve feet and twenty-five years away, the public bar had stood. It was there, precisely there, that it had begun, the conversation that would revolve on Arvon.

So what had brought Fairfax to this meeting of minds? Imagine a family of such bizarre dysfunction it's bound to impair the development of any youngster . . . other than a young poet. Let me save you the bother: grandmother (you note the tremble that has me mention her first), Irish and devout, whose holy water font she keeps primed with Paddy's; grandfather, English upstanding Cavalry hero; their children (Fairfax's mother, aunts and uncles), each an individual anarchy, a union of contradictory cultures, alive at a time which itself was all contradiction – the aftermath of the War, which on one side was life regained, and on the other the austerity of a morgue. That's where we find the boy, the grandson, the son and the nephew – Fairfax, already at fifteen a poet, escaping a war-torn family life, the heavy gauntlet of school, into a . . . breathing space. An alternative home. Maybe it too was a mad house – but for the young poet it offered daily constitutional sanity.

The two uncles were George and Kit – George Barker, the poet, and Kit Barker, the painter. They took Young John (as they forever referred to him) in hand, and became by and large his education. Not the graft of instruction (though in time George would prescribe ways of practice, and pass exacting comment on manuscripts and work in progress), but by opening their lives to him. For most – most people, most artists, most poets – acceptance of a vocation involves acceptance that the only conceivable fulfilment is that of total commitment. Very often this leads to confrontation with the conventions and priorities of home and social background. Not so for Fairfax. His acceptance into the family asylum, and then being allowed to follow as the norm the artist values and way of life of his uncles, had hugely eased owning his identity as a poet. If it also contributed to life's handicap, well there's the rub. As a teenager he imbibed (the word carefully chosen) the luminary Soho pub life – Dylan Thomas, Francis Bacon, Sidney Graham, Geof Burnard and all. Then when George and Kit went to contribute to the astonishing post-war creative foment centred in St Ives and West Cornwall, Fairfax lit off on his bicycle from London to join them. He soon learned that adroit beachcombing was not just a metaphor for the poet's craft, but a means of survival. The significance of this as background to our initial Arvon-directed conversation was twofold. First, that what he had assimilated was not hearsay, but experience first hand and well salted. Under George's fierce, exacting glare the work, the poems and day-to-day survival were knit to a single way of life, compact and lived to the full. And second, that this good fortune had made him the more aware of the deadening isolation experienced by many imaginatively gifted youngsters, young writers in particular, for whom there was no readily available affirmation or guidance from practising artists.

Irish grandmothers (I was able to contribute two), childhood in rural Devon haunted by the War, involvement with poet and painter, being sidelined into teaching, and so on . . . this grist of coincidence spooked our conversation. But the most improbable thing we had in common, and the one that as far as Arvon was concerned would be determining, was that we'd both been allowed the experience of working with accomplished writers. It was this that had left us, in my case at twenty-seven, feeling we had completed an authentic apprenticeship. From talking together we began to identify a shape to, perhaps even a formula for this initiation – one seemingly comprised of five stages or elements.

The following extract from my introduction to Fairfax's and my book *The Way to Write* tells how my side of the story was to contribute.

When I was five my father was killed in the War. I've realised only recently just how powerful the impact of this was – as if losing touch with his physical presence undermined the self-assurance that would allow my imagination to assert itself. In fact, as I now see, it went so to speak underground and I lost touch with the full force of it. So my years at boarding school from seven to sixteen were lived (call that living!) in ignorance of my creative self. On the surface I was fairly cheerful, and did what was needed to survive. It was only later I registered this as a time of fear and intense, unrelieved boredom. In fairness to the school,

I offered them only this surface to work with, but, for whatever reason, they did nothing to discover or put me in contact with what, beneath the surface, was a pretty formative imagination. What they did do, however, was impose routine training in the primary skills: reading, writing, a bit of Latin and a daily dollop of Prayer Book and Bible. Primary skills: the first element.

Every now and then during those years my inner life would freak to the surface. These invasions hit me with the force of self-recognition – moments of reassurance and the anguish of exile. Then at around sixteen came the phenomenal. One night at home I woke to find the room apparently alight. I sat up in bed and saw myself reflected in a mirror on the far wall. The light seemed to fade from the room. Half in dream, I was impelled to get up, fetch from somewhere in the house paper and colours (my stepfather was a painter) and make a painting of what I had seen – this boy, wide-eyed, sitting up startled in bed. When I looked at the painting in the morning I found I'd written a title at the bottom: 'Who's there?' As if the boy had heard an intruder in the house! I took the picture to school with me, and one day walked with it inside my jacket down to the modest art school. The art master had always attracted me. Like so many art masters, he created within the school system an alternative world with different and seemingly subversive values. With great apprehension, I showed him the picture. He looked at it for only a few moments, and then he looked at me with his unnerving directness and said simply, 'Can't think why you don't do more.' That was all it took, but perhaps it was the permission to be that had been denied me since the loss of my father. From that moment I dared to go underground, to where I found I was alive and startlingly confident. I started to write, but secretly – partly because for years the school had taught me that I had no conceivable aptitude, and partly because I was immediately aware that the working of the imagination as it would engage me was necessarily clandestine, well away from the scrutiny of the prescriptive. I began to hoodwink the system so that I spent more than half of my last eighteen months at school in the art school. The second element: validation of the individual experience of the imagination.

When I left school I was convinced I wanted to be a painter. I'd secured a place at Oxford, but having to wait a year before going up gave me the opportunity to attend art school. Then another curious story: our neighbour, an old general, remembered a 'young artist chappie' who'd served under him in the First World War. The General commanded. 'Young Kapp,' he said, 'I'll have him look you over. He'll know what's best for you.' 'Young Kapp' was then sixty-five – Edmond Kapp, distinguished painter and draughtsman. He was living in France, but by chance was due to visit London and was so amused by the General's orders that he agreed to see me.

I visited him at around eight o'clock on a beautiful June evening. Someone showed me into a small sitting room. I remember the shock as he walked into the room, the breath-catch. What he brought with him – the compactness, the energy – struck me as somehow lethal. He was quite small, Jewish, with eyes dark and brilliant and with a focused penetration that would have been violent but for the gleam of curiosity and mischief. I was suddenly completely unprepared, stripped of all my middle-class, public school politesse. Kapp had lived all his working life as an artist, and his work had drawn on and led him through an extraordinary range of experience. When he came into the room I was hit by a reality I'd never encountered before, that of the artist dedicated and answerable to the imagination, living on his own terms and open to life at first hand.

We talked for some ninety minutes, and because the reality I encountered was so unfamiliar to me I felt that I was in a dream. He asked me questions and seemed to listen to my answers with a curiosity they couldn't conceivably warrant. He spoke of himself, and of what being an artist meant to him. The more he said the more excited and apprehensive I became. He seemed to speak of an absolute asceticism, which, because his context was clearly a vividly picaresque life, and because it was in some way associated with the integrity of desire, confused me. In the end he looked with that same gimlet attention at my little portfolio of work. He said that he never taught because his time was too precious, but then said that he thought I did have a gift. He showed me his work, some of his wonderful drawings. Finally he said that if after our talk I was still drawn to painting, I could if I chose come and live near by for a while and work; that I could, for a fee, come and talk with him for three hours once a week.

That night and all the next day I was in shock. I felt utterly exposed. I felt exhilarated, lonely and frightened. I felt I was in a new territory – a place I'd always secretly wanted to be, but for which nothing I'd so far learned or been taught had any bearing. I felt that there couldn't now be any retreat from this place, but at the same time there was no guarantee I could cope with its demands. On the way home I stopped the car and went walking into the woods. At some point I was astonished to find that I was in tears (something not countenanced at my school); I didn't know whether this was relief at having come finally home, or the sadness of someone going into exile. By the time I got home I was better resolved. In fact, even then I knew dimly what had happened. Those ninety minutes with a person who spoke from his being as an artist was live information I'd never been exposed to. In him there was no division between experience, knowledge or practice. No division between means and ends, or between life, living and the imagination. Above all, no division between living and learning. I suspect I also realised that I'd come by this live information in perhaps the only conceivable way – not by abstract dictate in the hierarchy of the classroom, but simply in communion, workaday communion, with someone of lived and undivided authority. That evening I told my mother I no longer wanted to go to art school. I wanted to go to France and paint, and visit Mr Kapp once a week.

That's the third element: initiation into the integrity of imaginative practice. Perhaps what Van Gogh referred to when he wrote, 'As far as I know that word [artist] means: "I am seeking, I am striving, I am in it with all my heart"'.

Edmond Kapp was an extraordinary mentor. The house, his and his wife's, was full of painting, music, literature, argument and laughter. And everything – making an omelette, the relish of an anecdote, lighting a cigar, writing a letter – appeared to be unpretentiously but exactingly part of an artistry. I felt I was experiencing a liberation from years of grey self-denial. But then came a problem: Kapp was fiercely critical of any shortcomings in my painting. I began to lose my way. I realised I was unsure of what I wanted to do; I began to fear that I wouldn't 'pass the examination' that would qualify me for this way of life. I became depressed. But at the same time I began to write more, though secretly because I hadn't forgotten what school had taught me – that that sort of diversion was beyond me. There was a crisis: I couldn't paint any more. Then somehow Kapp got out of me that I was writing. He insisted on seeing the work and was immediately enthusiastic. Soon we were spending more time talking about writing than painting. The result was that by the end of the year I'd written a little book of childhood memories. An old friend of Kapp's was David Higham, the eminent literary agent. He sent my book to Higham, who was enthusiastic. So, at nineteen, I had a distinguished agent. The book came near to being published, but, thankfully, wasn't. Higham advised me that at Oxford I should for the time forget about writing and just live to the full being at university, which is what for the most part I did. I had outstanding tutors, including Nevill Coghill, but there was nothing I learned that had bearing on my own writing, or in any direct way on the practice or craft of writing. And it is significant that Kapp, for all his detailed encouragement, had not been a writer.

When I came down from Oxford I made the common mistake of thinking that if I went away for a year to write I could prove one way or another whether I was a writer. I wrote two drafts of a novel, which David Higham and his readers thought promising, but not ready for publication. I was (familiar story) suddenly nowhere – exhausted, depressed, helpless and, even among my friends, profoundly lonely. Then, again by chance, in London I met John Howland Beaumont, the deaf South African poet. Beaumont made a scanty living as an occasional correspondent to *The Times* and as an inspired copyeditor. He agreed to read my novel. He returned it with polite encouragement. When I pressed him for his opinion he said that it was fine but that I needed to learn to write. I was, to say the least, taken aback, but managed to bite back enough of my indignation to ask whether in that case I could come and learn from him. He agreed, and so a kind of apprenticeship began. I visited him in his small single room in Kilburn two or three times a week. Always we worked on something I had written, maybe as little as a paragraph. He concentrated exclusively on three things: alerting my ear to the difference between reporting and what he called 'writing at first hand'; the economies that allow accuracy in the essential art of writing by implication; and, for him I think the most necessary skill, a command of syntax. So entirely had these disciplines of elementary craft been neglected in my education that at first I was afraid I lacked any sense that was alive to what he demonstrated. But after a time – and he was patient, uncompromising and persistent – I realised with excitement that my ear was beginning to come alive. From the moment I'd begun to write I'd known that I had a distinctive ear that drew me to a certain music; I had assumed that was all the gift one needed. And syntax? The word meant detention and a Latin primer. For Beaumont, though, command of syntax was chiefly what enabled a writer to be a magician. Where there was the ear and the skill, syntax could be the fusion of cadence and meaning and narrative drama. It controlled the heart-catch. In any sentence it could make for the unfolding of life. And was as essential to poetry as to any form of prose. And for any writer was the key that would unlock the voice. I was sent away time and again to redraft. Gradually I became alive to what he was on about. And very gradually (in fact a process that has never ended) the new deliberation became seemingly more effortless, more spontaneous and, whether in description or mood or feeling, more accurate.

The point is that here was something that needed teaching – I had not been able to discover it on my own. Outstanding academic tutors had never touched on it, nor had Kapp, exceptional artist and precious mentor. I came to see (and this was to be the core of Fairfax's and my approach to Arvon) that the only person who can teach the technique of writing reliably is an experienced writer. That is because the teaching is proved by experience that is wholehearted and profoundly relevant. It is the authority that can relate the specifics of technique to the spirit of writing. Which means the authority in a specific art of one who has been 'in it with all his or her heart'. A Sufi writer, Mouni Sadhu, has said:

> There exists a mysterious spiritual siddhi or power which only a perfect master can possess. It is the ability, unaided by special words or deeds, to help and promote the evolution of his disciple's consciousness. It is actually unexplainable, but I believe it to be something like an invisible radiation that reaches to the deepest recesses of the disciple's soul. Then, if the man is able to tune this consciousness to the vibrations of the master's spirit, he knows many things that remain hidden for others.

My first experience of this was with Edmond Kapp; here the transmission, or awakening, related to the artist's total commitment. The second was with John Beaumont; and here the authority included and conveyed something specifically related to writing.

It may be that complete mastery is available only to complete authority. Even so, a limited mastery is also powerful, to the measure of its limited authority. Or at least that's the belief that Arvon is based on, hence tutors who are practising imaginative writers. Anyone who has worked in sympathy with a more advanced practitioner of his or her craft must have experienced what Mouni Sadhu is getting at. So, the fourth element: apprenticeship to craft in the full, live context.

The fifth element is practice. The apprenticeship over, then it's work on one's own – the whole package, which most often is the unfolding wrangle between survival and commitment.

*   *   *

Survival! Here were Fairfax and I, both intent on writing, both trying to meet the bills (in those days fees and random pickings for poets were even harder to come by) by teaching within a system of education which, as it seemed to us, we had survived only by good fortune. The schools we'd been sent to we looked on not just as penitentiaries but processing plants for the prevailing national culture. They operated the same purely functional education policy to shore up a dysfunctional society – one that viewed the imagination as a societal utility, as opposed to the faculty of genuine self-expression . . . of, in fact, genuine education. In particular we felt it was a system which, while allowing painters and musicians to teach as a kind of peripheral extra, removed literature from life by effectively denying the existence of living writers. And as for teachers . . . it would be some years before we'd simmered down enough to realise what for us would become one of Arvon's central tenets: that genuine teachers too were artists. But like the young writers that concerned us they were for the most part denied the self-expressive experience and the guidance of appropriate authority needed if they themselves were to be reliable guides to the imaginative development of their students. In other words, denied the training required for the fulfilment of their vocation.

But, as I say, that would dawn on us later. For now we were angry not so much about the way this system had treated us, as about the way it was still treating young people, conditioning the gifted to not take their gift to heart, and imposing standard drill that trivialised imagination to irrelevance.

On the beer-bench we rumbled on about this tyranny. But in our sober moments we were growing more restless about our inability, or was it just our failure, to do anything about it.

THE OPPORTUNITY

1968, the year the Revolution almost happened (Paris, Grosvenor Square, Hornsey), Fairfax's and my conversation was now into its sixth year. Antoinette and I had made home and a life well out of the way on the North Devon coast. I'd had a novel published, and a second collection of poems accepted; sufficient notoriety to be invited to a North Devon Schools' Poetry Day.

A building like an abandoned Fighter Command hangar. A bank of buses; from each school a busload of kids. In the chill hangar a vast circle of chairs – and by the time I showed up they were all occupied: more than a hundred 11–16 year olds. Well chilled. Each youngster sat nervous with a poem, not their own poem but somebody's poem, copied on to a sheet of paper and held in a shaking hand. And so round the circle, one by one, they read or muttered or stumbled. Chilled before they read, and afterwards frozen with boredom. And that was it.

'So what did you think of *that*?' the organiser asked me, breathless with self-congratulation.

The boasting on the beer-bench was suddenly in the past – I'd been fetched into the frontline.

'Awful!' I said.

'Oh,' said the organiser. 'So what would *you* do?'

A youngish hayrake of a man with ears like the handles on a harvest jug was walking past. He'd heard the challenge, and stopped to see what I'd come up with.

'I'll tell you,' I said – a rhetorical opening to allow me to check back to *the* conversation. Then, as if stating the obvious, 'The ones interested in writing poetry, I'd have them live it for real. Three or four days living as writers, with a couple of practised poets around to show the ropes and simply be on hand to help with whatever they might choose to write.'

'You're on.' This wasn't the organiser, this was the one with the ears. John Butt, newly appointed County Drama Adviser. He too had been asked to sit in on the day.

'You find the place,' he said, 'and I'll come up with the kids.'

'They must *want* to come,' I said. I think I was hoping for a way out.

'They'll want to come,' said Butt.

'You on?' I said to Fairfax that night on the phone.

'I'm on,' he said. 'But where?'

*　　*　　*

It reads like a roll-call of Johns. Next, John Lane.

Fairfax and I may have been the prime perpetrators, but the list of those without whose reckless abetment Arvon could never have got off the ground goes on and on, and if you relate it to Arvon's survival it continues to this moment. But it's also worth pointing out, since it's sub-text to my plot, that in today's restrictive practice there's no way Butt or Lane could conceivably unleash such a liberty. John Lane, a painter with furious energy in whose hand the sword of William Blake couldn't snatch so much as a nap, had a couple of years earlier been given the job of developing Dartington's new project in North Devon – a rural arts centre that would respond to, programme for and activate this extensive, little-populated, largely rural community; and above all celebrate its unique qualities and tradition. It was to become a model for a new and international means of arts promotion. The Centre was residential, beautifully but simply furnished, a renovated country house. Pretty much a lost village on a hill above the Torridge valley with views south to Dartmoor, and to Exmoor in the east. One of the first things John Lane had done was contact local artists and craftspeople of every description and ask how the Centre could be useful to them. So now I rang him and asked was it conceivable we could run our experiment at the Centre. What did we want to do? I told him. I told him we wanted to find somewhere the young people could be away from everything, schools, family, and radios – alone with the opportunity to write poems. Fanciful? I might have been asking to borrow a hammer. He said, 'The end of August all the staff are on holiday. The Centre will be empty. You can have it then.' I said, 'But you realise it'll be just Fairfax and me, and maybe fifteen kids?' 'You'll take care of it,' he said.

Five years later John Lane put hammer to nail – became one of the founding signatories to the Arvon Foundation Ltd.

*   *   *

Two years before this, in the autumn, someone mentioned that Ted Hughes was away from things, in a hut somewhere fifteen miles down the coast near Widemouth, working and on his own. I'd known he was in Devon, but we'd not met. I'm puzzled by what I then did – it doesn't seem to fit my pattern of behaviour. But there it is, an entry in my commonplace book, 13 November 1966, an extract from a letter to Fairfax:

When I got up it was a wet grey spiritless day, and the hump was too heavy on me for work, so I off in the car to the devil to see if I should run into Hughes. At Widemouth I walked on the cliffs for a time and looked at the zestless sea. Then drove into the village, asked a petrol man where the pub was and drove to it up the hill. I parked in the car park and as I got out a tall man was walking into the park towards the bar. I stood my ground and simply called out, 'Are you Ted Hughes?' He swung round as if someone had taken a swipe at him. For a moment my knees shook and I thought I was going to be dumb, not in awe of him so much as the happening. Strange that one never gets used to these presentiments, these encounters and entertainments of the spirit. We drank some beer and talked easily for an hour.

I found him impressive, with a towering turbulent presence, like an Ahab. He has the physical disposition to accommodate his driving demon – I felt it strongly, a Promethean character – steely, preoccupied eyes and jaw jutted to the devil. And out of him a slow gentleness, an unspeculating humour, a tried wisdom, and a soft, very beautiful voice.

Not bad for a first impression. One thing we talked about was the idea of creating a salient into the school system by enabling young people eager to write to spend a few days living as and working with experienced writers. As Ted would later write in his introductory essay (incidentally, an unrivalled statement of the at-onement of education, imagination and vital society) to Fairfax's and my book *The Way to Write*, he wasn't convinced by the idea. But at the same time there was the unguardedness, which he seemed to allow to just about everything except his own operational privacy, so that he could end by saying that if anything did come of the idea, he'd like to know. Which meant that when the Beaford experiment was a fixed date we were able to tell him, and he agreed to visit, and to give a reading.

There were so many individual contributions vital to Arvon's survival, but I think no-one would dispute that Ted's contribution was of an order all its own. From the moment on the last evening of the Beaford course, when he walked into the Centre and found the kids setting the table with flowers, and cooking the meal with the confidence of knowing the making of it mattered, and saw their luminosity, and the stillness of some brimming composure, and would have this confirmed a little later when before his own reading he'd listened to what they had discovered to write out of these days, his commitment to Arvon never faltered.

On Eric White's Arts Council Literature Panel Ted must have supported Fairfax's and my first application for funding. Thereafter there were few Arvon matters he'd not be involved with: little committees, ad hoc brainstorming sessions (he seemed to relish especially each new crisis), high and low level delegations. Endless times he and Carol, his wife, would open their house to meetings, or ask people in any way involved to meals. Arvon in the north was possible only because he made available Lumb Bank, the house he'd bought at a time he was thinking to return to his native landscape. At one dark hour when Arvon's debt seemed bound to bring it down, Ted faced the problem by dreaming up and then engineering the first Arvon International Poetry Competition in 1980. He persuaded Charles Causley, Philip Larkin and Seamus Heaney to join him as judges. More than 30,000 paid-up entries of unrestricted length, and the judges read them all. It was won by the future Poet Laureate, Andrew Motion. Probably Arvon should carry a permanent stigmatum on its escutcheon to mark how its survival drained the raw energy store of English, Cornish, Irish poetry – Ted said he wrote nothing for at least the next six months. But Arvon *had* survived. In fact it was in the black . . . for a while.

Ted himself never ran a course, but was the visiting reader on many. Often he would simply drop by, or attend the readings of others. No ostentation, no suggestion he'd gone out of his way. But that energy of his, again it was something else – his presence would have a magical effect, a contagion of imaginative excitement. Relate this to the entire field of his generosity and one can see how his association came to inform the operation. As his own identity evolved, became 'ennobled' by the Laureateship, this identification, remarked in high places and remote fishing lodges, did Arvon no harm at all. But to Ted life was all of a piece, a continuum of constantly awakening curiosity to be taken moment by moment. Each instance that took his interest became the object of an intense engagement. For Arvon this meant, as if by appointment, engagement with what some of us imagine was one of the overseeing mage intelligences and protectors of this nation's Writ.

THE FIRST COURSE

The First Evening
The Centre was ours. Fairfax and I were edgy as a couple of squaddies abandoned to hold the outpost against the enemy's advance. Fairfax was laying the table: I was to cook. We'd decided to go with this dish I did, Poet's Stew. I'd learned it from John Beaumont. He cooked it in his bed-sitting room in Kilburn, in a saucepan on his single gas ring. Potato, onion, carrot and scrag-end of lamb – simmered a long, long time. We weren't having these kids – that's if they showed up – being served any fancy ideas about life as a poet. Still it was the first night and this called for something a bit special. *Devonshire* Poet's Stew: that's Poet's Stew cooked in cider.

And then they did begin to show up. In total, fifteen – boys and girls, aged sixteen to eighteeen, from a range of Devon schools. They were delivered by parents or teachers who looked round the place and up and down at Fairfax and me, and went off wide-eyed and shaking their heads. Quite right. Imagine today suggesting to parents, teachers, local authorities, in fact to anyone, that they hand their young people over for five nights in an isolated rectory into the sole charge of . . . well, two young poets. To do what? To write poetry.

John Butt has now hung up his clipboard – but even if his career should be terminated retrospectively from that day, his persuasive powers would still surely be valued as a national asset. Mind you, all fifteen young people had *wanted* to come. They wanted to write.

During the meal we all kept well away from the subject, whatever it might be. We washed up, and then went into the sitting room for our introductory session, intended to make everyone feel at home. I was feeling homesick. Fairfax and I had decided to come clean; we said that we knew about them only that they were interested in writing – not so much what other people wrote, but in getting on with their own. We told them that we had that in common, and that the next days would be theirs, their own writing time. We said we were poets, and that the only thing special about poets was their belief that poems were important and that time spent working on poems wasn't a waste of time. And then we said that in our experience most schools, apart from the occasional marvellous teacher, were brain-dead to the real importance of creative writing and the circumstances required for producing it. And then we said we were there not because someone was paying us but because we were interested to see whether in these circumstances our experience as writers could be any help to them with their writing. And acting tough we said we had work we were eager to get on with back home and that if all this was a lousy idea the sooner we pack it in the better. And finally one of us said (and I remember how the words seemed to reverberate back to us, perhaps mockingly, from the queasy future) that this was an adventure that we were in together, and that if it and we did come up with the goods, then who knew? We might have fetched together something . . . well, unforgettable.

Before we turned in, the three lads from Crediton (Fairfax and I later referred to them with due reverence as The D-stream Baader-Meinhof Gang) took a walk, almost certainly to the bottles they'd left hidden in the garden hedge; and Flash and Stephanie – whose eyes had met over supper with a resounding clunk! – were irretrievably in love. When all were safely – safely? Yes, that I think is the word for it – in bed, Fairfax and I agreed it had on balance been an ominous and promising beginning.

Day One

We woke to our ownership of the world. The house and the countryside. Late August sun; all Devon's fields gold unto harvest, and near and infinite away in the woods the pigeons each in turn dreamily attempting and never quite able to remember how the line should end.

Breakfast – and after breakfast, I never knew why, Fairfax and I lost our way. I doubt either of us could ever have told you what a seminar is. But suddenly 'the voices of our accursed education' whispered that after the Poet's Stew a seminar was what was needed to get us back on track. So that's what we convened, a seminar on the grass in the Centre's garden. We did know that a seminar was serious business, and that one needed something pretty heavy to make sense of it. Prosody! We were five halting minutes into the subject of prosody when arrested by a groan as of a belly-ache. One of the Crediton Three had rolled on to his back and was glaring at the sky.

'I thought,' he muttered with menace, 'we were here to do writing.' It was 1968, don't forget: the tone with its whiff of cordite was hot from the barricades. Fairfax and I glanced at each other, and then nodded. 'You thought right,' we said. And that concluded the seminar. It was also, in my judgment, the moment Arvon came into being.

We spent a little time discussing ways of stalking a poem. How one needs first to come out from the shadow of what other people might think – to arrive on one's very own in the moment, and there be alive to its newness. Which, for the poet, means being alive in each of one's five senses. And then we said something about words – how a poem can say what we really feel only if the words are our own. Seeing one or two look apprehensive, we told them we wanted to be sure everyone was happy with what we were doing, and so we'd meet each of them briefly at some point in the day. We'd put up a list of times, and they could choose when to come. And we'd all meet together again before supper. We then drove to the shops in Torrington with the ones who'd agreed to be the day's cooks.

I don't remember what we ate that night – only the consensus that it was an advance on Poet's Stew. After supper, after we'd washed up, Fairfax and I said we'd like to share with them some things we'd written. I remember wondering, was it because they themselves had spent the day writing that their attention was so immediate, so completely given?

Day Two

Again the gift of summer and of out-of-the-way Devon: the oak woods, the secret meadows, the river, the glimpse of the distant moors. What had we planned? Nothing much. I think we sensed that four days was a shape already in place. In fact we'd already run out of time, and into some other sort of time, but one which knew what it was up to and would, if we trusted it, apportion the way.

So after breakfast we met and discussed for a while why sometimes a poem is reluctant to show itself. 'It needs you to come to it entirely on your own.' But why? We ran and re-ran the question, and finally agreed it might be simply that, where you're not on your own, it's hard for your poem to be in touch. We wondered were most people afraid to be that much alone – could that be the reason so few people wrote real poems? Maybe they felt it was like being asked to get lost. Maybe they were right. Maybe you need to get lost to arrive at yourself. Maybe that's the poem . . .

And that was when Fairfax or I, or the two of us in agreement, said, 'So today's your chance to get lost'. We suggested they went out and took some food with them. 'Go together if you like, but be on your own. Or if you stop indoors, be on your own. And the poem? Don't worry about it, it's already there. Be ready for it, keep your eyes skinned, sniff it out, listen . . . listen, try it on your tongue.' We said that if anyone was having difficulty getting lost, the two of us would be around to lend a hand. We told them we wanted them back.

They went off out of the house. Flash and Stephanie thought they should try getting lost together. We saw no-one till late afternoon.

We met together before supper. They were slow to talk, as if back from a long silence. So had they got lost? One after another simply nodded. Except Flash and Stephanie, who looked sideways at each other – whatever that meant. Had they written anything? They all had. 'Good,' we said, 'then tomorrow we'll get to work.'

Over supper they began to talk, and each had a story to tell.

Day Three

The third day was work. We met after breakfast, and again agreed we'd put up a list of times when each singly could meet and discuss work with the pair of us. Then a quick briefing. Redrafting, we told them, was perhaps the most creative part. We weren't there to tell anyone what to do – but if we could be alive to the poem they were after, then maybe we could draw on our store of experience to suggest ways they might explore. Craft, or the way of bringing words to life, was something you must develop an ear for, and that came with practice – which was why a more prac- tised writer could be a help.

And throughout the day as they came back and back, each time with a new draft, and as they were animated by the clarity that opened in their work, Fairfax and I began to realise that a process was working which, even though it was requiring every amp of our energy, was entirely beyond us. As we dimmed, so the place brightened with the kids' excitement.

After supper the pair of us sat back, and the students gave us a reading – favourite poems, or new discoveries from the load of books Fairfax and I had brought with us.

Day Four
In the morning, meetings again. Determining the final polish to a poem or poems. That was when Fairfax and I first saw what we'd witness so often at Arvon over the next thirty years – how the completion of a piece of imaginative work was the realisation of a deep-seated completeness. The imagination was not, as our so-called education had done its damndest to suggest, beyond us, but integral to each individual's self-expression.

Ted Hughes arrived at around six, and the young people read their poems in the sitting room. *Their* reading. Ted, Fairfax and I were the audience. Maybe the poems weren't more exceptional than every poem needs to be. But, as I remember it, there was a thread to them, and each one a discovery that enlarged on the discovery of those four days. Light from the poems seemed to filter into the room – the gleam of being young, of having been out in the sun, and handed the moon and given the key. The young people themselves – since their arrival four days before they looked more substantial, as if they carried more clout. And as for Flash and Stephanie, whatever it was they'd seen in each other the first night they now had something to get their teeth into.

When Fairfax and I had declared the last night's meal a full glad-ragged feast requiring our most accomplished cooks, the D-stream Baader-Meinhof told it straight: there was no-one else they would trust with the responsibility. So now while they basted the two roast chickens and tiddies and concocted a stuffing, and the rest set the table with white napkins and flowers, Fairfax and I took Ted down the lane for a pint in The Globe. In the pub Ted nodded slowly, and he too seemed to attend to what he was finding to say, not just about the quality of the young people's reading, but the register of the moment and the event – and the eventuality. It was, as the next thirty years would prove, his conclusion.

After the meal Ted sealed – and maybe he finally unsealed – the course with his reading. Those early poems – 'Thought Fox', 'Hawk Roosting', 'Bull' . . . To someone who never heard him, there's no telling what it was like. I remember thinking, 'Why on earth is this bloke so nervous?' Later I realised it was something else, more of a temper in the surrounding air that was trembling his shirt and his trouser-legs. In the room there was breathing – but whose? All the young people were holding their breath.

Some years later one of the Crediton Three wrote:

When we got back to Crediton total shell-shock set in for all three of us. We wandered around the streets not wanting to go home. We didn't go home for ages and ages and ages. We just sat around and talked about it for a long time. I think it had been a rather shattering experience. What would we now do back home since we weren't the same people. We had been called on to write as if writing mattered – and for the first time someone hadn't just put a tick or a mark at the bottom of one's writing. I think what was shattering was that suddenly *everything* mattered.

Nick Stimson. He'd go on to Rolle College, become an English teacher and a published poet. A few years later, he and his wife were the directors of an Arvon Centre. Since then much of his passion has been focused on writing and directing music theatre, making sure his excitement is contagious in schools and young companies, in prisons and communities. For three years he directed the National Student Drama Festival. Not that Arvon's claiming any of what he himself has done – only this, it did give him the opportunity to write 'as if everything mattered'. One of the poems he wrote as a sixteen-year-old on that first course ended like this:

> The dull thuds of realisation
> Echo around the allies of my past,
> And still the cry of my friends
> As they drown in the fear of themselves.
> People, stand up and shout!
> Tell nature how to live again!
> Tell the seas how to uphold the ships!
> Tell the men to stop crying!
> Tell everything, You're alive!

THE NAME

From the outset writers tutoring an Arvon course have usually found the experience unexpectedly fulfilling. However, I don't think I've met one who's not found it also unaccountably exhausting. Fairfax and I tend to feel complacent about this: that first course we not only tutored, we administered, centre-directed and were, twenty-four hours a day, *in loco parentis*. When after the end of the course Antoinette, with Fairfax's sons, Michael and Jo, came to meet us in Bideford, they walked past without recognizing us – we were disembodied with fatigue and gaunt as survivors returning after years in the gulag. And like those survivors, I guess, we had an informed disinclination ever to be caught by such an experience again. So what undermined our resolve?

Antoinette and I were invited to a local arts centre, to a discussion about art and education. A man who introduced himself as headmaster of a secondary modern school told a bewildering tale. Three lads from his school (three lads . . . for some reason I found I was bracing myself) who'd been able to spell nothing much other than trouble, had recently attended a residential creative writing course. And something had happened. I was about to push for the exit when the headmaster went on to say that when these three returned they seemed genuinely to have changed. They'd begun to apply themselves. I didn't like the sound of it – a diversionary tactic, the hallmark of the Baader-Meinhof, they were planning a coup. But the headmaster didn't leave it at that: the change in their attitude was having a beneficial effect on the performance of their entire year.

When we got home I rang Fairfax. We tried sharing the view that we'd never seen it as part of our remit to found a

New Model Society – but finally we breathed a deep breath and accepted that if something useful *had* come out of our experiment we weren't entirely free to do nothing about it. Once committed, it wasn't long before we were having to accept another thing, namely that far from it being us who'd lit on a bright idea, it was an extremely determined idea that had lit on us. In fact it was more like a spell out of control, and we a pair of sorcerer's apprentices bound for the next several years to try to cope with its magic.

We contrived a short report on the course, a little dossier of cautious intent which nonetheless claimed to have established a realistic way for writers to make, on their own terms, a live contribution to creative education . . . provided it were given due funding. And we sent it off to the Literature Director of the Arts Council. That's when the idea began to demonstrate its hold on its own providence. In the first instance the report precisely coincided with the Literature Department wondering whether, if they could come up with a way of employing writers in schools, this might not only be a respectable means of getting cash to writers, but an alternative to awarding grants on someone's estimate of merit which always caused such uproar in literary circles. Now suddenly there appeared on their desk a package, however limited, of relevant track record. And the second instance? It was the Literature Director himself, Eric Walter White.

Eric White was next in the line of those without whose individual commitment Arvon could never have got off the ground. He was an autocrat in a way that would probably no longer be possible, and a sublime self-styled enigma. A large clumsy-looking man whose way of being was sensitive and precise. His appraisal was exacting but full of warmth and mischief, and his regard for a person's gift seemed balanced by affection for their humanity, particularly if it were interestingly flawed. A transparent conspirator – but the conspiracy merely a means of determining precisely what *he* intended should be done. One felt certain that no secret was safe with him, but on the other hand that it would be safe to trust him with one's life. While he ran the Literature Department, his specialist interest was opera. As a chairman he would encourage heated, radical discussion, sum it up with an illegible but disarming smile, and disregard it entirely. Almost in secret, he wrote poetry. He was the most unguarded and engaging arts officer that I ever met. And probably the most committed.

Eric acknowledged our report by summoning us to London for lunch. An excellent lunch in a smart Italian restaurant. We were interrogated, expertly frisked for any meaty intelligence, hearsay, gossip, and with wine and benign transparency eased into indiscretion. But mention of our course didn't appear to be on the agenda. Fairfax with his across-the-green-sea gift of talking to anyone endlessly about anything was in his element. I, though, finally threw a tantrum, swallowed my cannelloni, and said I thought we'd come all this way to discuss our initiative. Eric beamed at me as if after all I might turn out to be an interesting oddity, and asked what we would do if we were given some money. We said we'd arrange a number of similar courses run by other writers and see if the same thing happened. Eric clearly thought that that was enough on the subject. He settled the bill and shooed us gently but firmly on our way.

A fortnight later I was staying with Fairfax, lending him a hand with a schools' poetry anthology he was editing for Longmans. Mid-morning, we were in his study when the phone rang. Fairfax went into the kitchen to answer it.

'Eric, hullo,' I heard him say. And a moment later, 'Eric, that's tremendous news.' And then, 'That's not a problem. We'll let you know.' And then, after a longer pause, 'I see, so could you just hold on one moment.'

I heard him put down the phone, and then he ran into the study, like a man who's woken up past his deadline.

'Quick!' he said. 'They've given us the loot – but they're not handing it over unless we have a name. They need it right now.'

A name! Where, just like that, does one find a name? In a study, with books? In a book! There was a book open on his desk – and he grabbed it.

Fairfax at the time was working on his sequence of poems, *Adrift on the Starbrow of Taliesin*: hence the book on his desk, *The Mabinogian*. Page 426, the Notes. He focused, and in a spooky séance-like voice began to mutter, '... Taliesin, Chief of the Bards, presided in three chairs, namely: Caerlleon upon Usk, the chair of Rheged, at Bangor Teivy . . . but he afterwards was invited to the territory of Gwyddnyw, the son of Gwydion, in Arllechwedd, Arvon . . .' He looked up. 'Arvon,' he repeated, which was a relief to me because Arllechwedd could have been a mouthful. 'Arvon,' he said it again on his way back to the phone. And I, sitting there, a spectator a little bemused, thought the word sounded a shade skint. An enrichment leapt unbidden from my tongue. 'Foundation,' we heard me utter.

'Eric,' Fairfax, a little breathless, pronounced down the phone, 'We have it, a name: The Arvon Foundation.'

The loot, if my memory can be believed, was £200 – and the conditions were that we run four further courses, *Arvon* courses, the following summer.

John Lane renewed his support by agreeing that these courses too could be run at the Beaford Centre, and on the same generous terms. John himself had taught at the radical education centre, Bretton Hall, and had in his own words 'written about and practised education through art, and knew about its practice backwards'. In fact there was something almost dismissive about the way he viewed as self-evident what Fairfax and I imagined we were stepping into the radical unknown to prove. Which makes the point that, while Arvon's way of involving writers was innovative, at the same time it was merely adapting the time-honoured tradition of master-apprentice craft training. And also that the impulse behind it was very much of its time, in fact just one other expression of the 1960s 'break out', when consciousness was being challenged to make new contact with the wider imagination, and on so many fronts to rediscover the primacy of experience over theory and dictate.

Yes, but what about other writers? If there were to be other courses, we'd need to sell some of them the idea. With the fee we were able to offer (£25), *sell* is perhaps an understatement.[1]

It's a primary Arvon mystery how Fairfax and I, who have a focused inability, in fact it often seems a perverse disinclination, to sell anything of our own, were together or singly, unfailingly able to interest people in Arvon. Were we on this one subject granted a gift of tongue? Or was it that some pre-

---

[1]. Arvon today, from the funding it has attracted, is able to pay its tutors realistically. It has always resisted any suggestion there should be other than a standard tutor's fee.

ternatural Arvon control led us always to the people who, whatever we might say, would suffer a contagion of if not committed interest then undeniable curiosity?

On this first recruitment drive we braced ourselves with the notion, particularly in relation to the fee we had to offer, that we were assembling some sort of Magnificent Seven. We called first on Michael Baldwin at his home in Richmond, and under the very pear tree that features in one of the funniest poems ever written (his account of how he put his National Service experience to use in a counter-assault on this fat pigeon who was stealing his fruit), and after a couple of glasses of white wine, we propositioned him. He took our shilling. Then to Alan Brownjohn, Michael Hamburger, Peter Redgrove, Jeni Couzyn, D.M. Thomas, Jon Stallworthy . . . perhaps not all of them everyone's idea of a gunslinger, but metaphor was part of our business.

Curious they might have been, but they were still cautious about what exactly was being expected of them, what they might be letting themselves in for. We told them, 'It's as if it's your home. They're staying because they want to write, and they want your help. They lend a hand with the house and the cooking, but what you do to help them is up to you.' But that wasn't enough. If they were signing up for four days, they wanted more detail. So Fairfax and I went away and composed the proto-version of Notes to Course Tutors.

Again there's the mystery, though it's one that's become more evident as the years have run by. Isn't it quite strange how much of what has remained constant in the shape and content of Arvon's courses was simply what happened by chance, or the invention of necessity, or perhaps some ghostly prescription, on the first course? Five nights, four full days ('Long enough, but not too long,' we'd say with sage hindsight). Fifteen students. Two writers as tutors and a visiting reader. The resident tutor's reading on the evening of the first day, the shared 'anthology' reading on the third. The shared housekeeping with its unforced two-way inference that the everyday is both context for and enlivened by the imaginative life – and which works on the understanding that the need to write is acceptable. And so to the creation of a safe writing-house to which each person is given the key.

But writing our Notes to Course Tutors we realised we wanted to convey something of which we were as yet only tentatively aware. The transformation the young people on the first course had seemed to undergo suggested that this had been more than a course of instruction. They'd been illuminated by the experience in its totality. Together we'd all found a shape to the four days that seemed to draw on some archetypal way of self-discovery or dream quest; so that the completion of a piece of imaginative writing with its attendant sense of fulfilment was the outward sign of an inner realisation of completeness. What would become the core tenet of Arvon had already defined itself, namely that without imaginative expression the experience, or gnosis, that gives individual and formative value to education, is absent. The experience of one course was the confirmation we'd both been looking for – that imaginative practice and its training were at the heart of genuine education. The rest of the world could argue whether Arvon was an arts or an educational venture. But Arvon (and I think every writer who was happy working with Arvon was alive to this) would know that whether it was running courses for primary schools or teacher trainees, open courses for adults or courses for writers, it could only be singly both. For the pair of us the word education had rediscovered its meaning.

So our Notes, as well as being detailed, tried to present the days as four stages in a complete journey or adventure. The first, the preparation, and attentiveness to the departure; the second, the opportunity to break with the habitual world, to be on one's own, to be silent, to give oneself to the imagination; the third, concentration on practice, the tutors' guidance on how the work is responsive to craft; the fourth, the polish, bringing the work to completion, 'knowing the place for the first time'.

However, what had come clear to us on the first course was that of the four days it was the second that was pivotal. Time and again we would see people, often coming from years of wanting to write, who when the opportunity was finally given them suddenly realised they were afraid. So often because the opportunity they had devised for themselves suddenly became a self-imposed examination they were likely to fail. To talk about writing, to attend workshops on form and technique, to discuss the things in their lives that made it impossible ever to devote themselves to writing . . . no problem with any of that. But to do the one thing that is absolutely needed, namely to be fully on one's own without prospect of interruption, and totally dependent on one's imagination . . . that's frightening. This 'getting lost' was the one thing Fairfax and I insisted on. And to help them we'd most often remove ourselves (often, dare I say it, push off for a game of golf). And what we found, almost always, was that these few hours of 'being on one's own' were what ensured that the white-heat intensity of work on the last two days was reliable, founded and genuinely self-expressive.

I remember a striking example of this. A middle-aged woman came on one of our courses, eager to write poetry. She arrived exhausted from a front line job with children in care and, as she told us, from the recent break-up of her marriage. So agitated in fact that at our first meeting, whenever she asked a question she'd instantly answer it herself, belittlingly, as if this were what she expected from us. It didn't seem a useful meeting. The next day, the second, before Fairfax and I left the students to being on their own, she visited me. She didn't know what to do with the day, and wanted guidance, which I found difficult because her agitation and speediness of mind were as before. I don't know what possessed me: desperation or perhaps a vague instinct, probably both. I said, 'Today is your day, but I'm asking you to do one thing for me first. I want you to find a ditch. (It was a beautiful summer day, and Devon has many ditches.) Then find your place in the ditch, the place of your choice. Then be in the ditch for exactly three quarters of an hour by the clock. For the first quarter of an hour just be there. Then in the remaining half-hour identify in the ditch five objects or happenings each of which will act as an image, one for each of your five senses. I think you'll find that's the way into a poem.' She nodded, and not very steadily went on her way.

When Fairfax and I returned, she was the figure waiting at my door. I saw immediately that something, maybe something dreadful, had happened. Her face had that fine, clarified look of someone emerged from a long spell of crying. 'So,' I said, all business-like, when we were sat down, 'how did it go?' She started to cry again, not hectically, in fact calmly, the last measure of the weeping. Finally she said, 'We were married for fifteen years, and I now realise I never saw him. I never looked at him.' Neither of us said anything for a while, and then I pointed to the sheet of paper she had in her hand. 'You've written something,' I said. 'Am I allowed to see it?' The poem was simply a record of her time in the ditch. What she had touched, heard, sniffed, tasted – and what she had seen. A wonderful poem, with depth to it that took one's breath away. Coming to, finding oneself in a ditch: a metaphor for the beginning of life? Well of course, what else?

A thing we never thought to do was to tabulate the role of an Arvon tutor, or prescribe the ways he or she should work. To be a grade-driven instructor, or a professional teacher within the system, training in 'classroom skills' is clearly required. But we'd seen how, when a practised artist responds to someone genuinely seeking his or her guidance, an individual engagement is involved for which training in the conventional sense is not relevant. What's referred to here is something other than instruction – more like the transmission of the authority that comes from knowledge of working with the imagination, and which affirms the responsibilities, rigours and 'entry upon hallowed ground' that this involves. For this to be effective a certain openness, maybe one should call it sincerity, is required in both tutor and student – and in the tutor, as well as experience, genuine commitment and, as far as possible, the suspension of self-concern. It wasn't long before Arvon had confirmed this. A tutor might be hesitant, shy, gauche with a group – and yet, when it came to the individual meeting, the thing itself. In fact so much was this the case that one of Fairfax's and my bad dreams was of the virtue gone out of Arvon because some bureaucratic overview, to suit its own book, had required tutors to be trained, evaluated and certified.

Then there was a question of the workshop. The current definition of workshop isn't altogether clear. In one sense – I'd say the true sense – it encompasses the essential operation of any art, which can only be where practice is always a learning, a way of discovering, and, driven by the imagination, a self-determining gnosis. In other words a form of education. Perhaps education itself.

By this definition Arvon, like any genuine arts training, is nothing other than a workshop. But the word is also used to describe an instructive, practical group meeting, discussion or workout. It wasn't just our moment of self-betrayal in the Beaford garden the first morning of the first course that had put us on our guard. We'd both experienced (for instance my stint in America, connected to a university creative writing course) how groups could be hijacked by dominant personalities, performers and powerful egos. And how these could be used to impose certainties of approach, taste, technique, style – and so favour some aptitudes and disregard others. This seemed to us precisely not what Arvon was about. I guess our interest was always with the shy authentic gifts, the unique voices that these workshop certainties and generalities would tend to disregard, thereby undermining what little confidence they possessed. So in our Notes for Course Tutors we did emphasise the value of the individual as opposed to the group meeting. In time we would learn that here too there was no general rule, and that indeed there were tutors wonderfully gifted in bringing to the group an excitement that would be catalyst to each individual imagination.

Now, forty years later, in universities across the country there are some fifty MA degree courses in creative writing. The opportunities on offer for quality guidance and for extensive practice many will find wonderfully attractive. All universities, though, since they select by means of an examination system, are unapologetically exclusive institutions. They would doubtless argue that they merely select out those who won't benefit as much as others from what they choose to provide, but this means there is always an imposed, and to some extent imposing measurement of success. Since it bears on reputations and careers, it could hardly not be prescriptive; it is possibly also proscriptive.[1] This is where Arvon does stand apart. It is, militantly if you like, non-exclusive. Its door is open to anyone interested in exploring their gift to write[2] – and much effort has gone to building a bursary fund to ensure this remains a reality. Arvon exists to encourage whomever to explore their own needs and their very own means for imaginative self-expression. If, along with all the excellencies of Arvon's success stories, this quite often results in writing that's not so well behaved, then so be it. Some of the Arvon work I remember best is raw as a blood-print scratched on the wall of a prison cell. Asked to defend these values I no longer bother to attempt it – easier just to tell the story of Nick Webber.

I was on a day residency in a school. I was detailed a group by a blitzed teacher who clearly saw here an opportunity to draw breath. And for her to draw breath meant I was given Nick Webber. Nick was perpetual motion with a mind of its own. He

1. The current (Trinity 2005) issue of *Oxford Today* magazine trails the launch of the University's Master's degree in Creative Writing: 'The two-year part-time course will combine intensive development of writerly skills with high-level critical analysis. Students will also undertake a placement to gain experience of writing in the real world, for example with a literary periodical, a theatre or a literary agency.' Does that sound like a one-stop

didn't decidedly try to prevent anyone else achieving anything, he just existentially made it impossible. I did what I could during the morning: not much. After lunch I came back determined everyone should have time to write. 'You too,' I said to Nick. He sat down at a table, and before he could move I put my hand on his head. For half a minute I had to apply pressure to keep him in his seat. Then quite suddenly he let go, or whatever it was let go of him. He became still. I felt through my fingers, and so somewhere in his head, the dream pulse begin. Next thing he was writing, racked by the concentration and energy it required.

A Nothing
A Small smelly Nothing is in Braunton.
It is 5 foot in height.
And it is 110 pounds in weight
And it's a good thing
And I went and said to the Nothing
'What is your name?'
'It is Nothing,' he said to me
And he said, 'what is your name?'
'It is Nick and I am a friend to you.
And will you be my friend too?'
'Yes,' he said, and me and Nothing
Went to the shop and Nothing said
'I am your FRED.'

You may think, as I did at first, that FRED is a mis-spelling of friend. But there are two reasons for thinking it may not be so. I told him I liked his poem very much, gave him my address and

catch-all training camp for operatives, aimed at softening up and cornering the literature-as-industry trade? A threat to Arvon? On the contrary, an additional incentive – so long as Arvon is in touch with its original concern.
2. Arvon has always had similar 'open door' policy for selecting its tutors (one independently published volume being the sole requirement) – which has enabled Arvon to survive in the minefield of literary sectarianism.

asked if he would kindly send me a copy. It arrived a week later, and on the page in the margin were two drawings: a sort of speckled beaky monster, and a very friendly dog. The monster has in front of it a tiny drawing of what looks like a poem on a sheet of paper. The title is clear: NOTHING. The dog also has what looks like a poem on a sheet of paper. Title: Nick Webber. I still spend time (the poem, framed, is conveniently on the wall of our lavatory) wondering who is who. Is Nick Webber the dog, or is he the monster? Or is the beaky monster perhaps 'the Beak' – the face of his accursed education? The one who awards the marks: Nothing. Nothing, Nick Webber, NOTHING! But I've decided the dog is FRED. And the second reason is that to have the layout and punctuation so correct he must have had help from his teacher. And with everything else correct he surely wouldn't have mis-spelt friend. One other thing: he must have been pleased with his poem to have managed to stay still long enough to write it out again.

I still have the feeling there is something profoundly true about this poem. And as with many masterly poems I've never quite fathomed it or tired of it. And if it is true, uniquely true, is it, John Keats, not also uniquely beautiful?

Behind the day-to-day details and whatever else we tried to convey in those first Notes to Course Tutors was a twofold inference. Firstly, that the tutor should be open door to the student's discovery of his or her unique gift, and to guidance in the way of its expression, and the rigours of craft and practice that this would demand, and to the reality of what Vincent Van Gogh meant when he said that to him the word artist meant, 'to be in it with all one's heart'. Secondly, whether the outcome of all this for the student was the distinctiveness of a secret journal, or a best-seller livelihood, they were equally not the concern of Arvon, or of the tutor, except in as much as they were what the student wanted to write, and written in the understanding that 'everything matters'.

THE GREAT LEAP FORWARD

If conversation was the beginning of Arvon, then Robert Gathorne-Hardy must have been in there from the start.

Bob was a writer who lived in a village called Stanford Dingley, in a majestic mill house full of first editions and fine ninteteenth-century watercolours. On one side of the house was the River Pang; on the other, directly across the road, was The Bull. The Bull was where Fairfax and I took beer most nights when I was staying with him. Bob was in residence at The Bull, as far I could see, every night. He sat up high one end of the bar in Bob's seat, drank mild from his special pottery mug, and did the talking. If anyone else should manage to get a word in he'd seize on this as opportunity to thrust alarming assignments of snuff up his nose which, after a few moments, would explode, often with significant dis-gorgement of blood, into a large white-spotted red handker-chief. A conversation of whatever complexion happening within the scan of Bob's hearing he would, quite firmly, appropriate, and then lead down wayward avenues until those he'd fleeced were found listening, with the expression of deep-trance subjects, either to the judgments of his esteemed mentor, Logan Pearsall-Smith, or to accounts of intimacies in the twilit margins of Bloomsbury. And while it's difficult to write about Bob without making him sound like a character out of Pickwick Papers, he was actually a serious and com-mitted writer. So, no question, Bob was in at the start.

Even before Arvon was constituted, Bob had assumed the Presidency. From that moment his contributions would prove undeniably formative in both style and content. Among the first of these was his agreeing to host in The Mill House Arvon's first designated Young Writers' Course. This was to be the showpiece of our Year Two programme – and clearly crucial in that Eric White himself had elected to be there to observe, along with, and so to speak from up his sleeve, a mystery potential funder.

The follow-up programme Fairfax and I had devised was intended to test the original findings, but at the same time to explore whether the formula could have wider application. There was a second schools' course at Beaford, run by Peter Redgrove and I think Philip Callow – complete with Peter's unleashing of imaginational dynamics including (I heard years later from one of the students) a séance during which an amenable Chinese spirit dictated a poem; and concluding with (the course, not the séance), a reading by Ted Hughes. There was a writing course for Dartington drama students whose aerial disregard over five days of the need to wash up brought John Lane almost to his senses, and hence the whole venture to the verge of collapse. And then Fairfax and I ran the first course for teacher trainees – from Rolle College in Exmouth.

We remember this for a number of reasons. Firstly, we arrived to find the place deserted – no-one was there, and no-one arrived. It finally emerged that this was a result of prudent economics – Fairfax's. We were scheduled by this as-new diary he'd found that related to a year in the 1930s but whose dates coincided with the current year – or had until the end of February when the presence or absence of leap year had introduced a glitch. We were a day early. The next day the students, in spite of our prior insistences that they must want to come and write, arrived hesitantly. There was a batch of four grotesquely injured young men. One had a Long John Silver-style wooden leg, two were on crutches and all were in bandages, splints, slings. They entered supporting one another and looking like the troupe of mutilated mendicants in the little painting by Pieter Bruegel. Fairfax and I found nothing in this more challenging than anything else. The final afternoon, when we were all easing up with a game of cricket on the Centre's lawn, Fairfax and I realised first that we'd not seen our injured for . . . well, for a long time; and second that this was because they'd recovered and were now prominently involved in the match. They confessed that the idea of spending days in a writing retreat had sounded so bizarre that they'd armed themselves with what seemed like a good exit strategy. But after a few hours had felt able to dispense with it. The fact that the pair of us hadn't noticed was seen as hallmark of poetic myopia. The more significant transformation was in their, in fact in all the students' evaluation of being given time to work on their own imaginative expression. Two of the walking wounded were so far converted that they were soon helping us to run the courses.

But for us the enduring impact of the course was this first glimpse of the capacity for creative fulfilment that resided untapped in these emerging teachers – clearly every bit as essential to their complete being as it had been the previous year to that of the young people from schools. We would have it confirmed time and again on Arvon courses over the years. But it was then we first surmised how vast must be the store of teachers' creative energy lying dormant throughout the country. Given expression, it could become the authority needed to nurture individual creativity in schools. It was though so clearly being disregarded, even proscribed, by the system – with the result that many teachers were becoming demoralised and unfulfilled.

During the first years Arvon was able to programme courses for teacher trainees largely because the colleges included in their curriculum an 'activities week', which gave opportunity for actual experience of some endeavour related or complementary to the intensive training syllabus. Repeatedly heads of departments, as well as the students themselves, confirmed that the 'short, sharp shock' of working imaginatively with a full-time practitioner seemed to amplify capacity and confidence and often be a major catalyst in a student's whole development. In time there was further evidence of this in that teachers who had themselves been on an Arvon course were those most likely to be insistent that their pupils be given some similar opportunity.

Before long, however, the increasing pressure of the training curriculum saw to it that even these limited opportunities for self-expression vanished. Some thirty years later Fairfax and I were asked to run a course for teachers at Arvon's Yorkshire Centre, and found ourselves face to face with the full-time constraints that current practice placed on any form of teacher self-expression ('But presumably you manage to read?' 'Read! Oh yes, in the last three years *To Kill a Mocking Bird* thirty times: it's on the syllabus.') As a result a group of us came together under Lawrence Sail's chairmanship, and launched Tandem. Conceived as a teacher/artist alliance, it aimed simply to extend the formula Arvon had employed over the years by providing opportunity for teachers to explore their own need for imaginative expression by working with experienced artists in relevant disciplines; and opportunity for artists on their own terms to involve themselves in education. A success? At least it lit another candle in a dark place. One teacher, after taking part, wrote, 'Tandem is the first initiative I've come across that recognises the centrality of teachers' creativity to their role in education'. And incidentally it highlighted why schemes to introduce into education some sort of artist-led practice that bypasses involvement of the teachers tend in the long run to be counterproductive – they further undermine teachers' self-belief with the inference that 'doing creativity' is something they're not up to, which leaves teachers only further out of touch with their own potential. And so the system's primary resource for nurturing the creativity of young people (one might call it the nation's future) is put cruelly out of service. The encounter that happens on a Tandem retreat is two-way, a mutual recognition that at its best amounts to an exchange of identity – and so is healing and productive far beyond policy-led schemes to introduce artists into schools. Here Ananda Coomaraswamy's frequently quoted dictum, 'An artist is not a special kind of person, but each person is a special kind of artist,' takes a somersault, and when it has picked itself up and dusted itself down, finds it can be read another way: 'A teacher is not a special kind of person, but each person is a special kind of teacher.' These concerns are, and have always been, integral to Arvon's whole concern.

Completing our Year Two programme of research and development were a couple of out-of-Beaford courses – intended to establish nothing less than the pan-national relevance of the Arvon formula! One was held at a kind of artists' commune that Fairfax had stumbled on near Bognor Regis. He ran it with Michael Baldwin, and they had Alan Brownjohn to read, but they remember only that it was probably a success, this on the substantial evidence that they themselves survived. And then there was the showpiece course, the Young Writers' Course at The Mill House, Stanford Dingley.

Everything looked promising. Eric White had disclosed that the mystery funder we needed to impress was Cal Younger, secretary to the Chase Charity. They were to be lodged in the moth and dust comfort of The Mill House. To be truthful, there was one thing that didn't look so promising: we were having difficulty assembling a quorum of young writers. To be more truthful, we were having difficulty recruiting even one young writer. Fairfax and I weren't generally given to worrying – but here was a worry.

Once or twice already we'd had to rely on the Baader-Meinhof Trio to act as our rent-a-student outfit. On this occasion though they were able to supply only the two: Nick and Horace. Fairfax had an inspiration: he persuaded Graham Fawcett, the Literature Director of the then Southern Arts Association, to shift roles from observer to participant. On my way up from Devon I tried to persuade a hitchhiker with the air of one on a vision quest that he'd thumbed himself a lift to Parnassus – he was initially enthusiastic, but passing Swindon he returned to earth and began to worry he might miss connection with his girlfriend at Dover, of which he had pressing need. And so we were left with the three.

The students and guests arrived around six on the Friday evening. Bob immediately let it be known that six was the time he thought of going across the road for a drink. Eric and Cal must have accepted this as the requisite induction for Young Writers – they led the way. And then? Well, I'd say the evening, through to closing time, was a success; in fact a fairly standard Friday night in The Bull.

Next morning, not too early, Fairfax's and my schedule was supplanted by a session of literary discussion, reminiscence and gossip. Between Bob and Eric. Bob would lead, but any pause for an implosion of snuff and Eric would have the floor. The Young Writers, and I think we should include Fairfax and me in this, nursed our hangovers, tried to look attentive, and in the art of innuendo, and of the spiced presentation of hearsay from literary sources, were powerfully enriched. At midday Bob drew the line, and announced that this was the time he thought of going across the road for a drink. Towards closing time a taxi arrived to take Eric and Cal to the station. Eric, in his goodbyes, shook hands warmly with the Young Writers, congratulated them on having been selected for so prestigious an event, and treated each to beaming acknowledgment that could, but probably shouldn't, have been taken as indication of almost certain future preferment. I don't remember what happened to the course after that . . . it was however Saturday, and I'm not about to suggest The Bull was closed on Saturday nights.

The Young Writers' course was an outstanding and quantifiable success. Within six weeks the Arvon Foundation had received a renewal and increase of grant from the Arts Council; a grant from The Chase Charity to employ a part-time Course Director; and a grant from Southern Arts to cover the region's involvement in a couple of courses. The future beckoned. We decided a similar course should be run the following year.

ENTER TOTLEIGH BARTON

The next John was John Couth – Arvon's first salaried officer. He'd been one of the walking wounded on the first teacher trainee course. When he'd shed his crutches he had found himself knocked off the path by having his gift for writing taken seriously, and was soon intent on discovering whether it held anything in store for him. Well, Arvon's part-time Course Director for a start. His job was to shop, supervise the cooking, and see the tutors felt at home. As well as helping us to recruit further courses to fill the projected expansion of the programme (eight, I think, in the third year).

So there was another summer, with the courses continuing at Beaford. But now Beaford had begun to develop its own residential programme. It finally dawned on us that Arvon, if it was to have any permanence, would need a home of its own. The question was aired at talking-shop level in The Bull. Fairfax and I were detailed to approach the National Trust with a partnership proposal we felt they couldn't refuse. We were right: they offered us tenancy of a majestic crumbling pile about the size of Blenheim Palace; and they said that we were what it had been waiting for, a Foundation with the means to restore it. The new dawn was put on hold.

Couth meanwhile was thinking of going for broke – and by the shortest route, which would involve finding a backwoods cottage where he and his girlfriend and her young son could try in the long term their taste for Poet's Stew (no, this isn't another sad story – before too long he'd become a full-time and, I don't doubt, wonderful teacher). He'd arranged for several estate agents to send him details of their market in lost cottages. At breakfast on the last morning of the course Fairfax and I were taking that year at Beaford, smiling Couth slid in front of us a specification that had been included with the latest sheaf of For Sales.

'Your Centre,' Couth said.

One could understand why it had been sent. A quick glimpse of the photograph, and it did appear to be of a small-ish thatched cottage. But the details told a different story: a lost pre-Doomsday, thatched manor farmhouse with out-buildings. Even if we had decided to look seriously for a place to buy, we . . . I mean not even we would have started here: a centre no-one would be able to find, and with the appearance of little more than a cottage. However, the photograph did seem to wink at us, and the place wasn't far from our way home, and on the morning after a course the call to get lost was undeniable.

Mr Miles had the key. We followed him down a distracted Devon lane, and then a deranged track. Over the hill and down. We drew up in the yard of Totleigh Barton, opened the car door – and recoiled from the stillness. Not silence . . . still-ness. Late August, somewhere past noon. A mile away across the river someone is calling, the sound catches up in the sun-light, and is the history all-told. Swallows veer to nest under the thatch eaves. A cow somewhere. A couple of pigeons swoosh over the thatch ridge, stall away sideways with a sudden clap of wings. A bee now and then murmuring past to check out the vine on the back of the pigsties. And then the in-dwelling still-ness, the containment, the complete preoccupation. Totleigh's abiding still. Stop any Saturday morning, ten minutes after the last of the others has left – and it's there. Not for the taking. But if it's partaking you're after, then here is open house.

Mr Miles unlocked the door and left us to find our way. Room to room – kitchen, dining room, hall, sitting room and upstairs – everywhere still and, just out of earshot, breathing; inhabited by its own completeness, a long-lived acceptance of what is past, or passing, or to come.

Mr Miles came to tell us he was going home, and could we return him the key when we were through. Through? We weren't sure whether what we were already through to could conceivably be anywhere. But we could tell we were beyond bounds from the first-time fact that we had nothing to say to each other. Maybe our thinking was that, beer-brave in The Bull, we'd put down a marker, never suspecting that providence would take it seriously. And now, recognising the precision with which providence had joined up the numbers in our dream-code sketch, we were losing our nerve. It was impossible. Yes, but was that really true if, however dimly, it had been conceived? And if we were to just walk away from what we had conceived, that would have to be the end of it. To continue the search would be feeble, a form of perfidy. We looked at each other, shrugged, and moved towards the car. But then stopped, turned back and walked around a bit more. 'I think I'd better ring Antoinette,' I said. 'She'll tell us to pull ourselves together.' So that's what I did, from up in the village. I said to her later, 'So why did you come?' She said, 'It was your voice – I thought I'd better come.'

It took her an hour to drive over. Fairfax and I sat on a seat in Sheepwash square and thought of things to say. I said, 'That's the thing about women, down to earth. Luckily. We'll be able to get on home. Stop for a drink.'

We left Antoinette to find her own way round. When finally she joined us, she did have both feet determinedly on the ground. She looked at the pair of us, and then in a down to earth way she said, 'Yes.'

Next morning I rang the agent. The property was under offer, pending a survey. I said, or rather I heard myself say, 'We don't want a survey, and we'll pay the full price.' Which seemed reasonable – after all if the place had managed to stand up for more than a thousand years . . .

Twenty-four hours later, a phone call: we were told it was ours. Our response was instant and level-headed: barmy. We were barmy. A centre down a lost track, no-one would find it. No-one would fund it. And then . . . what about the money?

Maybe we could just about have raised it. Antoinette's father, like mine, was a soldier. Both majors, both at thirty-five killed in action in the War, when both of us were five. And we'd both received, untimely and in trust, what was coming to us. But buying Totleigh Barton . . . the National Trust might have thought the Arvon Foundation sounded promising, but we knew the facts. And then a fortnight later the money was delivered. Or rather it was fetched on Antoinette, from property in Italy bequeathed to her father. Just like that, not so much out of the blue as out of sky that had begun to assume a rather ominous glare.

So it was Antoinette who bought Totleigh Barton. From James and Sheila Murray. They'd bought it three years before from Old Sparks, as everyone around remembered him. Farmer Sparks. The ruin of his old cart is still there beside Hal's writing hut. Totleigh had been a working farm in the old season-by-season sustainable style; but wasn't to be sustained much longer, in fact was already showing some signs of falling down. James and Sheila had begun very sensitively to restore it. James was a major mathematician. He taught in New York, and that paid enough for the family to go frequently to earth back in Devon. Until elected to a professorship at Oxford on a salary so reduced they were bound to sell. When they learned what we had in mind for the place, a home for Arvon, they did something astonishing – they knocked 10 per cent off the price. The impact of this was twofold: first, we'd have enough money for equipping the Centre; and second, we could no longer wax feeble wondering whether we'd done the right thing.

A deep breath, and we informed the Arts Council – or rather we rang Eric White. 'And where are we to find your centre?' 'Central,' I said determinedly, 'central Devon.' No hesitation from Eric. 'Splendid,' he said, 'I look forward to my first visit'.

On the train for London. Antoinette, someone else and myself in a four-seat compartment shared with a man carefully withdrawn behind his broadsheet. The broadsheet quivers from time to time, but there's no turning of a page.

I say, 'The poets, where are you going to put the poets?'

Antoinette says, 'The best place for them is the pigsties. It should be relatively quiet.'

The broadsheet quivers, then steadies itself.

'Yes, that's good,' I say. 'And the visiting writers, where would you put them?'

Antoinette gives it some thought. Then is decided. 'Only one place, the goosehouse.'

As the man gets to his feet he folds his paper. Making his way down the aisle towards the buffet car he gives the impression that the sedate carriage is lurching quite perilously.

September 1970 sees the completion, contracts signed and sealed. The following April, Arvon's first course in Totleigh Barton. For those seven months Antoinette was in charge. Equipment, furniture, furnishings, linen, crockery, cutlery . . . every detail that was needed for the Centre to open. It was the stripped pine era: a couple of quid for an upright chair, ten for a chest of drawers – each of them beautiful. Carpet for the sitting room and stairs; the curtains she made herself. The Monk's Chapel had served Farmer Sparks as a corn loft, with an outer hatch door. We replaced this with a window, and then uncovered the stairs down to the dining room that someone way back had bricked in at the base. The stair cavity was full of old corn. The old lime ash floors? Pottery tiles in the kitchen, and in the dining room and hall the beautiful grainy slates, £1 each from the reject pile of a crazy-paving quarry on the outskirts of Delabole (Derek Coish was laying the last one as the first students walked in). And outside the immeasurable manpower of Derek Hockin and his sons Brian and Paul, converting the pigsties, the goosehouse, taking the old rotten stalls from the barn, laying the floor, bolstering the roof.

There was one problem we seemed unable to solve; where were we to find the table that would be at home in the dining room? A table big enough. Wherever we went we'd ask auctioneers and dealers for clues as to that table's whereabouts. We were shown fine scrubbed farmhouse kitchen tables of good size but never with enough presence for Totleigh's dining room. We saw massive oak refectory tables, but with hauteur and price tag above our station. And then far side of Devon an off-the-High-Street dealer in Honiton told of a dealer somewhere in the sticks who had a barn out the back full of all sorts. We trusted the lanes and found it at last . . . with no-one at home. We tiptoed round the back into a silent yard of cobbles and cob barns. In one there was a pony with a blanket over its back, still steaming from a canter. As we turned to go a chicken with word of a new egg came squawking out of a window above the door of this other barn. In Devon one needs to take note of this sort of summons. The door was padlocked, but above the lock was the hole for reaching a finger through to the inner latch. Through it Antoinette could see, half-covered by an old sheet, under paint pots, flower pots, an old withy basket and a fair crop of onions, a table. A great table of two lengths of elm, three inches thick. It was, it had to be the table.

We rang the dealer that night. He said it wasn't his; he was storing it for another dealer who seemed to have forgotten about it – it might be for sale. It was for sale, not far off the price of the rest of the furniture together. But since it was the table, it was hard to think of an option. It had come, so the dealer told us, from the kitchen at Woburn Abbey. Fetched from afar! It sounded like dealers' talk. But then someone visiting Totleigh later said he'd seen another just like it . . . in the Longleat kitchen. Made it sound like early eighteenth-century Habitat. Thick elm on a pine base, a well-tried working surface, part butcher's block: all that Totleigh required.

We never thought there might be a problem getting the table into the house – not until the afternoon it was delivered. But that afternoon the window frame in the dining room was being replaced by the Hockins – which meant Hockin brawn was on hand to lift the table and slide it through the window gap like a drawer into a dresser. Good fortune? We didn't dwell on it – it seemed that with Arvon and Totleigh Barton this sort of service was pretty much standard.

In April, a fine spring evening, when the white minibus arrived with the group of teacher trainees from Culham College, the candles were burning on the full-laid, flower-decked table. The wine uncorked, the smell of the meal throughout the house. One end of the hall Derek Coish was laying the final slate, and upstairs in a bedroom, down on her knees, Antoinette was giving the wondrous oak floorboards one last polish.

ESTABLISHMENT

Now we began to take ourselves seriously.

When the grant arrived that would enable us to employ a full-time administrator Fairfax and I suffered an inflation of institutional self-esteem. We rang the regional HQ of Lloyds Bank in Exeter and announced that The Arvon Foundation was considering opening an account, and could the Manager set aside time to discuss this? The Manager stood as we entered, but then felt for his chair and slowly sat down again. He moved swiftly to his second thoughts and asked some recondite question about the nature of our Foundation. Our answer had immediate effect: we were back at street level, queuing with the rest of the down-to-earth.

Our advertisement attracted a deal of interest, but the job description reduced this to a manageable six applicants. Fairfax and I shortlisted the lot, and set aside a whole day for each of the interviews. At least we did for the first four. The fifth we met at Exeter station, assessed over coffee in the station buffet, and forty minutes later put, along with what he made no effort to conceal was a new lease of life, on the train back to Paddington. The sixth we cancelled.

The job was wrenched from our grasp by a friendly middle-aged couple. They quickly bought a house near by, and committed themselves for life. It wasn't a good appointment. No-one could question the quality of their commitment – it was when they revealed in full what they were committed to that we saw we had a problem. They viewed Totleigh Barton as the ideal centre, away from the world, where all comers might achieve moral advancement and abstinence – something to which the practice of writing, if under strict control, need not be an impediment. A course taken by Michael Baldwin, very much the Porthos of the Arvon Musketeers, soon exposed even more of a problem than we'd feared. A meeting was called. Fairfax and I persuaded Bob that his presidential command alone could manage this crisis. 'What do you want me to do?' he asked. 'Fire them,' we said, 'amicably.'

A long meeting. Fairfax and I maintained critical silence. Bob, every time he strayed from amicability to somewhere approaching the point, would need to steady himself with snuff. There'd then be a pause while he coped with a nose bleed, and the track would go cold. Finally the administrator must have decided he could take no more of this bloodshed. 'I think,' he said, 'it is being suggested we tender our resignation.' Before the amicable Bob had time to deny this (fortunately he'd been taken by a paroxysm of sneezing) Fairfax and I were on our feet and, like Monsieur Hulot at the funeral, were congratulating our late administrator and shaking his hand with the utmost cordiality.

My memory suggests that there followed a time when a mist settled over Arvon's in-the-field activities. No-one had been impressed with Fairfax's and my first formal appointment – neither the process nor the product. We were told by funders and friends, very firmly, that we must set up a reliable management committee. Eric White agreed to chair this for the time being: he was also Chairman of both the Arts Council and the new South West Arts Association Literature Panels, but the world seemed to accept that this was unlikely to threaten any conflict in Eric's interests. The committee identified among the original applications what might prove a safe pair of hands, Peter Mason's. Peter accepted the job on his own exacting terms which included being able to live with his wife and young family some thirty miles away. But his hands did prove safe because, through turbulence and mist, unconstituted Arvon survived – probably the most reliable and, from several points of view, interesting account of just

Top: A rare image of Ted Hughes and John Moat on Lumb Bank terrace in 1969.
Above: Ted and Carol Hughes, summer 1971.

John Moat beachcombing in 1971.

John Fairfax beachcombing in 1971.

Left: Henry Williamson, John and
Antoinette Moat in 1970.
Centre: Kit Barker.
Below left: Eric Walter White.
Below right: Tina and David Pease
with Ted Hughes.

OPPOSITE
Above: Totleigh Barton,
early morning.
Below: The Totleigh Barton Table.

George and Christine Tardios.

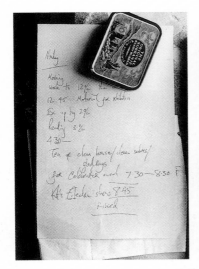

Above left: Fairfax's orders for
the day, for a writing and painting
course taken with Kit Barker.
Above right: The writer's gazebo
at Totleigh Barton.
Centre: The slate at Totleigh
Barton (mended).
Right: 1975 Totleigh Barton
Open Course: Alan Brownjohn,
Douglas Dunn and Gavin Ewart
with students, including Arthur
Elliot (left), founder of The
Friends of Arvon.

Jemima Burrell, Centre Director, cooking with a student.

how, is the Annual Report and Accounts 1972–73 to be found in full as Appendix 1. Mason administrated, but didn't wish to be involved with the actual courses. Someone was needed to manage the house and the courses – and out of the mist, very much as if mist were his element, emerged the providential figure of Alan Rodford. Where did he spring from? I don't remember, or maybe since I think of him as trailing paranormal tendencies, it is simply a mystery – like the Pied Piper without the vengefulness. He was well- and dark-suited with brown suede sneakers – not tall, but with the imposing air of someone who moved within circles. In constant attendance was an equally self-contained though less well-suited dog. The pair of them took up residence in Totleigh Barton, and soon were able to harness the mist as their ways and means. Together they kept the programme going. Though almost certainly to Rodford this was just another sideline, along with the robust medieval banquets which, according to rumour, when there wasn't a course, he organised for local yeomen. His dog would attend readings, grumble when they went on too long and, perhaps with poetic licence from Robert Frost's old dog, pass critical comment 'backwards without getting up'. When the mist cleared the pair of them vanished. Only to reappear punctually and again out of nowhere when the emergent Lumb Bank needed someone who knew the ropes. Rodford had a quartermaster's knowledge of the ropes. The other day I came across a letter he wrote to Fairfax telling how he'd located no more than quarter of a mile from Lumb Bank an unused cricket pitch, complete with changing facilities and a heavy roller.

Meanwhile, away from the front, progress was being made towards the establishment of a command post. We undertook this after Eric had in the manner of a gentle suggestion told Fairfax and me straight that Arvon must seek registration as a charity and a company limited by guarantee. A what? This

was when we established what was to become standard
Arvon practice: when at a loss, try your neighbour. In this
case Ronald Duncan, poet and playwright, who lived over the
hill from Antoinette and me. As suggested by the title of his
autobiography, *How to Make Enemies*, Ronnie was a self-
proclaimed malevolent. But we got on well, probably because
we knew his weakness. Ask him for help or advice and he was
unguardedly generous. Years later his Literary Foundation
would give Arvon significant funding. At the beginning it was
his guidance. He sent me off to Isador Caplan. Isador was the
man for the job. He'd set up the Maltings for Benjamin
Britten, with whom Ronnie had collaborated, and subse-
quently The English Stage Company which Ronnie co-
founded. He appeared have a key to the Charity Commission,
as well as a gleam, probably from both his diamond-tipped
mind and his excited interest in the arts. He set to work on
Arvon's behalf, and became Arvon's next unsought benefactor by trimming his fee.

One glance at the draft constitution and we realised that
the Fairfax/Moat autocracy of the backwoods was at an end –
though we would continue to contribute whole-heartedly and
remained, as will be shown, on call for special operations. But
now we had to identify our Chairman, which meant someone
who could make head and tail of the constitution. We called a
meeting in The Bull. It was the same idea, only this time it was
Bob's: 'There's this neighbour of mine . . .' A week or so later
Fairfax and I were called to The Mill House to meet Hal
Hudson, to tell him something more about Arvon than Bob
had told him already.

Hal was senior in Lloyds of London – would soon become
its Chairman and be knighted. His presence was daunting –
youthful, groomed, severe and powerfully charged. At the
beginning of the War, fresh out of school, he was determined
to be involved where the action was most challenging. As a

paratroop commando he went before D-Day on a special operation behind German lines, and was critically wounded. The field surgeon had given up on him – but then noticed how this throwaway of fragments gathered itself and determined to make it on to its feet to pee. The surgeon saw that here there was a will he could do business with, and changed his mind. Somehow Hal was got back to England, and put together again more or less – the less being a stretch of intestine, but none of the determination. I never gathered what, after the War, drew him to the City – only that whatever he'd chosen would have had to submit to his uncommon, steely integrity. His regard had a way of calling one to attention – not physically so much as in one's consideration of things. And it could be that he achieved this with Fairfax and me even under conditions of engagement that were Bob's hospitality. So the pair of us weren't tempted beyond the simple facts. Hal listened, and at the end gave an economical nod, and set out to walk home.

We'd been dismissed. Fairfax and I didn't take personally our unbroken success in putting Arvon's case – we assumed it was down to the power of the product. If our run had been broken it was Bob's fault – he'd pitched us out of our league. And we were wrong. Bob told us a couple of days later that the economical nod meant that Hal had agreed to be involved.

Why on earth? We would soon learn that beyond that steely regard there were other things alive. Like the sensibility that at Rugby had won him the poetry prize. Like his enduring love for poetry that was one of the things he shared with Fatty. Fatty? Well his wife, Lady Cathleen – but whom from the start we were licensed only to call Fatty (probably made possible by the fact she was anything but). Like the sudden humour that would break out of him, often quite boyish and, when he and Fatty were together, elementary. Like the unsought and entirely self-dismissive generosity with which, out of view and more than once, he himself rescued Arvon from terminal deficit. Like the parental irresponsibility that, a couple of years later, would have him, together with Fatty, entrust their mercurial, beautiful, tough little loony sixteen year old daughter to Fairfax and me, to drive to our first Starting to Write course at Lumb Bank – Louise, who in her own time would become a poet, Arvon Centre Director, committee member and benefactor.

So Hal and Fatty joined the line of those but for whom Arvon would not exist. And if what we were all witnessing with Arvon was part of some alchemical design, then for a time Hal and Fatty as the Royal Coniunctio intact seemed to ensure universal well-being.

The Arvon Foundation Ltd . . . the articles and memoranda were finally presented for signatures in November 1972. The signatories, along with Antoinette, Fairfax and myself were Robert Gathorne-Hardy, John Lane, Havelock Hudson and Eric Walter White. Company registration was achieved on 13 December, 1972. The first meeting of the Council was held on St Valentine's Day 1973. Hal was in the Chair.

THE LURE OF THE NORTH

For a time, established Arvon seemed even less likely to survive our efforts to sustain it. We persuaded resourceful friends (Christopher MacLehose, publisher, Andrew Lawson, painter and photographer, Charles Lenox-Conyngham, youthful captain of industry) to join the Council – but before long those with the business acumen we hoped would shape a solvent future were briefed by that same acumen, and staggered away shaking their heads in disbelief.

The story here becomes that of a ship in a gale being boarded by pirates who in the end throw off their sanguinary aspect, and reveal themselves to be the good pilots. George Tardios and Guido Casale. If their names imply hot-blooded adventures to a mere temperate Brit, just let him wait till he meets them face to face with their danders up. Which was where their danders tended to be. And yet each was responsible for introducing to Arvon one person (i.e. the two people) who would come to comprise its operational heart, and sustain it not just through some immediate crisis, but through the steady-state formative crisis of the next twenty-five years.

George Tardios, with his intense bird-of-prey countenance, had first shown Fairfax and me his menace on a course the pair of us were running for Rolle College. The first four days, after his breakfast (sometime in the afternoon), he'd taken up position in the dining room and each time Fairfax or I passed had followed us with his glare as if defying us to ask him what he was up to. Something which, glare or no glare, we wouldn't have thought of doing. But the final evening, he must have crashed through some barrier in himself – he was up all night working on a memorable poem. Next morning, while the minibus with all the other students was waiting to leave, he hauled first Fairfax, and then me, into the garden for his due of tutorials.

The upshot was that George became the first Arvon fundamentalist, and nothing would ever be quite the same again. He was now writing poems, writing well but with a weight of self-doubt so exacting it needed to be portioned out for treatment from any other available writer. Maybe it was this that led to him and Christine, his lissom wife, being installed at Totleigh Barton. But the actual circumstances are in the mist zone. Wondering whether George himself could help pinpoint the event, I rang him last night. We discussed this, as well as related matters, for more than an hour, by the end of which mist had been downgraded to fog. But what seems most likely is that when Peter Mason left to better himself, George and Christine moved into the house to manage the courses – and Rodford and his dog were put on the road to drum up business. It would be wrong to say George assumed control by degrees. He assumed control. Then, with a fundamentalist in charge, one who did his karate workouts in the barn and who over supper spoke of the outstanding schooldays' vendettas that still required his attention, we could relax? Not entirely. On the one hand Arvon was promoted more forcefully than ever before, on the other it appeared that tutors thought to have deviated from the book were lucky to escape with just the corrective glare. A Tardios report suggested that the chin of one deviant had erred so far as to brush the knobbly part of his, Tardios's, hand. But then the energy was lively in every department. Another legend tells how fur flew when Christine cooked for George's late breakfast the succulence from the fridge that was the prepared dinner of Frieda Hughes' ferret.

If Totleigh was the Arvon kitchen, the heat was now intense, and Antoinette and I managed to sidle out of it for seven months: an adventure with our children in the USA and Mexico. I don't think I ever fully caught up with what was happening when we were away, but by the time we returned, the pans were boiling over on the stove. During our phone conversation, George reminded me that he and Christine had been thinking of moving on for some time. But – and it was then the mist cleared a moment before settling even more densely – had elected to stay on to champion the fundamentalist cause in the glare of a revisionist threat. The threat had two facets: one that the Arvon operation would move to Lumb Bank (see how one gets befogged in a mist – George's tenure must have extended beyond my brief and into the historical phase of Arvon) which George countered by himself arranging so many courses that the case for remaining with Totleigh became undeniable; and the second from a politicised faction in the north that was planning a coup which George, on his account, sternly repulsed. It was also a time when, particularly in its new Centre, Arvon contracted a rash of disastrous courses. The door had been opened to a hoodlum element of writers who saw this as entrée to not Kubla's but Sir Toby's pleasure dome. But this too is on the record, and that's where I'd better leave it.

But how this situation clenched until other people thought it might be time for George to move on, no-one is able to remember. George though, as a matter of fundamental or fundamentalist principle, was not now about to budge. Totleigh became, effectively, his bunker. Christopher MacLehose, then my 6'6" ex-SAS publisher who'd allowed himself to be involved with Arvon, was staying with Antoinette and me. When he heard this news he ground his teeth and said, 'Right! I'll just drop over and sort this business out.' Hour tottered after hour. Antoinette and I kept apprehensive watch on the southern skyline. Christopher, when he returned, looked ominously serene. 'What an engaging chap,' he said. 'I stopped for a cup of tea, and we got talking.' There, in a nutshell, was the problem.

The fact we were all so fond of George was a serious headache. Still, finally, after what he decided was appropriate punitive action (he hid the mailing list which was discovered twenty years later under the oil tank), he and Christine moved on. Back in London he was promptly called on by the Poetry Society to oversee the first National Poetry Competition, and had soon published a book of fine poems which, and I still value it greatly, was dedicated to, among others, Fairfax and myself.

I was talking earlier this year, not long before wretchedly he died, to Andrew Goaman, the fine Devon farmer who himself had owned Totleigh Barton for a short time before selling it to the Murrays – and in the midst of whose land the Centre, but for its narrow causeway, is an island. For thirty years he'd had these oddball writers in the middle of his farm. Probably told his friends, 'Never thought I'd be into the rare breeds business!' There were occasions, if for instance students wandered off bounds, when in the manner of a North Devon farmer he would 'give it to us straight', but never obstructive, never a cross word. Did George help with this? Not impossible, because what I was suddenly hearing Andrew say with a stutter of laughter that sounded like an old Fordson starting was, 'That George, get on, he was the best of all the lot of them.'

And the best thing George (or perhaps anyone) ever did for Arvon? He decided he needed someone just a few hours a week to help with the typing. So he advertised in the local paper. The one applicant? Julia Wheadon. Julia. Julia and Noel. True to the Arvon principle of calling on the neighbours . . . they were the neighbours.

Noel and Julia – even by 1960s standards, they were free spirits. They'd acquire a ruined house, move in, restore it and move on. Their house East Totleigh was, much as thirty years later it is today, nearing completion. So Julia was a 'temp',

was she? For the first few years we simply valued her profi-
ciency, and were in awe of the way she kept to her agreed
hours and herself to herself. But as the seasons passed, each
with an increment to the programme, and the estimated completion date of East Totleigh remained a constant two years
ahead, we began to develop an alarmed dependence on the
detachment with which Julia allowed Arvon's perpetual white
water to tumble past her. Would she stay? As we held our
breath, so we noticed that detachment was evolving into her
own form of constancy. We dared to wonder whether East
Totleigh weren't becoming a bit like Penelope's tapestry: the
day's progress dismantled each night. Until now . . . now
there's no-one who's ever been fully engaged with Arvon's
unfolding labyrinth who would see her role as anything but
that of Ariadne: the provident abiding still centre that holds
the clue to the clue. Company Secretary, Senior Administrator, Arvon's enduring witness, register and memory store. For
care, caring, heart-care and detail she has always been her
own, but increasingly Arvon's, standard. From welcoming the
apprehensive student to meeting the Minister, she's been the
source of Arvon's confidence, and maybe the reference point
of its distinctive ability 'to care and not to care'. It's possible
that she contributed as much as the as-yet-unmentioned
David Pease to the integrity of Arvon's way of operating.

I can just about resist furthering the Ariadne clue by suggesting that Noel was the Minotaur. Not that he would be
short on strength. In a sense Noel is what Arvon got with
Julia, but it's a precise sense and not one that has anything to
do with conventional employment. It's more as if when he
saw Totleigh, and then saw the bunch of dreamers who'd
taken it on, he accepted resignedly that he was going to have
to shoulder the practical business of looking after the place.
I'd guess Noel is foremost among Arvon's unacknowledged
assets. On self-imposed standby more or less twenty-four

hours a day for more or less thirty years. If the cleaner's ill, the water's broke, the drain's blocked, the roof's leaking, the lights are fused, or some loafer's looking for an earful, Noel's suddenly there with a bag of tools and seemingly all the time in the world. He's there red as an apple (tribute to his legendary intake of scrumpy), drawing distinctively on his pipe as if intent on fetching the tobacco itself up the stem into his fumatory, and his stiff moustache active and cyclical as the brush on one of those new-fangled gutter-sweepers. A brush with Noel . . . not many students or tutors have been spared; in fact it's like a standard Arvon extra that doesn't appear in the brochure or the bill. Another complete education. You run into him and he's already talking, but how the subject arose, and where it's heading, and what it's about, that's none of your business. If it were you'd now be well briefed on whichever shenanigans . . . Shenanigans? That's what it seems usually to be about. Shenanigans in the Police Force (of which he was once a member), the confederacy of part-time wrestlers (of which he was once a member), the Freemasons, the second hand car trade, the planners, business big and small, the Hatherleigh Mother's Union (and I wouldn't be surprised if he was a member of that too). You may not grasp precisely which, but it won't matter because each is merely a metaphor for The Great Shenanigan. You stand there, out of your depth, mesmerised – until you can't take it any longer.

So that was a large part of George Tardios's legacy. What then of Guido Casale's?

If written into George's demeanour was a possibility of imminent eruption, in Guido's it was more a probability. You remember in comics those round anarchist bombs, the fuse sparking and down to the last quarter inch? One had the feeling that in the low life expectancy surrounding the Medici court he'd have found a deal of summary business. He had applied for the job that went to the safe pair of hands, Peter

Mason. At his interview the needle on the seismometer shot off the register as he assessed for us Arvon's bourgeois credentials. Fairfax and I were impressed by this show of firepower, and would probably have offered him the job. But following the catastrophe of our first appointment, the new management committee saw to it that on the new interview panel we were a minority. Besides, Hal made one thing clear: if Casale were given the job, that would be the end of his (Hal's) involvement. So that was that. Except it wasn't altogether.

I couldn't rid myself of the hunch that someone had an appointment with Casale, and that if it wasn't Arvon perhaps it was me. I invited him to stay the night at Antoinette's and my place. He agreed, which, given that he'd failed the interview, was generous. That evening I took him and a couple of bottles of beer up on the cliff to see the sun go down. We talked a bit – and then we got talking. About Arvon, about poetry, about William Blake, and about the fire that was locked in the flint. And then, until the sun went down, we talked some more about Arvon. Fairfax and I may have been wrong, but we hadn't been that wrong.

The upshot was that at the next meeting the Arvon Council did agree, finally, to the proposal that Guido Casale, funded by a pittance from the small San Giorgio Trust, which at the time was in Antoinette's and my control, should undertake a four- to six-month research project – to establish whether Arvon could have a future in two regions familiar to him, North Wales and North West England.

For a time we heard not a thing – but suggestions that the funds might be being laundered by some militant tendency were words to be eaten. On time, Casale's report was delivered. It was the works – startlingly thorough, incisive and positive. His conclusion was that the north west in particular might offer Arvon a fertile plot. And on that surmise he'd even made prospective contact with key people.

Here, in turn, was Guido Casale's legacy. He'd opened the door to the north. And the one who came reluctantly through it would prove the surety of Arvon's future.

Still some work to be done though. How was this achieved? The short answer is, Arvon-style. Fairfax and I were sent north as a scouting party. A person Guido had approached was Harland Walshaw who'd worked with John Lane at Beaford, and was now running (if memory's on beam) Fylde Arts. He helped convene a meeting in Burnley with representatives of various northern regional arts associations, including Yorkshire, Merseyside, Lancashire, and from North West Arts a focused-looking individual with even for the times an impressive out-reach of brown hair, by the name of Pease. Fairfax and I outlined what was moving in Devon, and the response there'd been from writers, funders, education people and students. We'd been alerted to the short shrift we could expect if we appeared as colonialists from the fatted south, and so we explained that Arvon saw itself not as an imperialist power, but as facilitator of a simple but effective operation which, having already Arts Council backing, might be useful in other regions. We wondered how would they feel about supporting the north's own Arvon Centre? 'You have a centre in mind?' they asked. Firmly in mind, we assured them, and if they were to consider supporting it, then it was merely a question of identifying the centre on the ground. This was met with an impervious north-ern demeanour, which we interpreted as encouraging.

On our way back south came a moment we would not forget. We'd been silent a time, watching the countryside reconvene somewhere the safe side of Birmingham when Fairfax said, or I said (you can choose the authorised or the revised version), 'That one with the hair and the direct way of looking . . .' 'You mean,' he said/I said, 'the North West Arts man? You mean Pease?' 'Yes, him. He was impressive. He'd be a good person to run Arvon.' And we left it at that.

I have the letter from Ted Hughes that came through a few days later – saying that Arvon could use this house of his outside Heptonstall, Lumb Bank. Antoinette and I had visited when he and Carol were wondering about a return to his native landscape. As a centre for Arvon ... mightn't it be, well, perfect? On the margin of Brontë country and the Howarth Moors, and yet within a radius of sixty miles, lived more people than in the whole of Australia and New Zealand together (or is that another bit of fiction?). We wrote to the powers in the north a fairly casual 'as we indicated when we met' letter.

So that's where we had our next meeting in the north, Lumb Bank. Ted and Carol were there and, to bring some boardroom sinew to Arvon's delegation, Charles Lenox-Conyngham, who was then Managing Director of a shipping company in Liverpool. This time the arts association representatives showed a different sort of wariness – as if the current here might be stronger than they'd expected. They gave Arvon at Lumb Bank their provisional support.

Suddenly there was a case for a National Director. Yes, but funded by whom? I imagine we looked at one another and then turned our heads in unison to see what expression was on Eric's face. Good, it was Eric's version of the Sphinx's smile. In a day or two he would recommend that we apply to the Gulbenkian Foundation.

There was a meeting at Totleigh Barton to discuss the appointment and job description of the National Director. I remember the atmosphere of corporate misgiving when Fairfax and I said we thought we knew just the man for the job, someone we'd spotted in the north with a good head of hair and this direct way of looking. 'Why,' someone asked, 'do you suppose he wants the job?' We didn't have a straight-forward answer to that, but no-one could see any harm in sounding him out. So I rang him. And David Pease said that as a matter of fact he had decided to leave North West Arts but that working for Arvon wasn't what he had in mind. Nevertheless to send him the job description.

His application was impressive on account of the strenuous terms in which he made it clear that he really didn't want the job, and didn't think he was the man for the job, and wasn't convinced that a National Director was what Arvon required. He was shortlisted. At the interview he repeated what he'd said in the application only with even more impressive conviction. By now everyone was struck by his consistency, vehemence and judgment. He was offered the job, and after a lengthy reiteration of his views, in the form of an affecting gallows' speech, had fallen on deaf ears, he accepted.

In March 1975, David Pease became Arvon's National Director. With that Arvon's stranger-than-fiction phase was brought to an end. The rest – veritable and verifiable – is history.

AND THEN

But I can't quite leave it at that. Besides, since the magic continued, I wouldn't want to break the spell.

Recently I heard the founder activists of Greenpeace inter-
viewed on the radio. They told how when the French agents
blew up their *Rainbow Warrior* in Auckland Harbour, and
outrage around the world resulted in a downpour of funding,
something changed. Suddenly the organisation had to be seen to
be respectable, and accountable to all manner of constitutional
demands. The whole purpose of the operation had been to challenge the establishment, but now it was being manoeuvred to
within the establishment's surveillance. As far as the founders
were concerned it was freedom from accountability that had got
the operation off the ground, and allowed them to feel engaged
in the first place. Now spontaneity and (I think they too used the
word) magic were no longer abroad in the same way, and
although they acknowledged that what had happened had to
happen, they could no longer feel engaged to the same extent.

Familiar story? So much so that it might define a phase in
the standard evolution of an imaginative venture into a work-
able institution. As administration becomes established so
inevitably the energy that went exclusively to furthering the
vision begins to leak to the new requirement of having the
operation comply with the constitution, and of maintaining
the property and the administrative costs and so forth. A
reality kept mostly under wraps is that there is a critical line
which marks when the leak has bled the operation of its life
force or, put another way, when voracious institutional self-
concern has consumed all the seed corn.

The reason I mention this is because it highlights another
freak of Arvon providence – it rubbed from the ring an

administrator who promptly gave the above formula the lie. How David Pease achieved this is a mystery, the more so in that for the first couple of years he continued to spend precious constitutional time berating the Council with how much better the organisation would be without him. Until finally he lost heart – lost it, that is, entirely to Arvon.

David's gift involved a recklessness of commitment that is itself unaccountable – not with regard to the relative peripherals of finance and constitutional compliance, but in the core formative matter of . . . well, himself. For twenty-five years he would remain unaccountable in the absolute dedication of just that: himself. I don't quite understand why this should have constituted the liberation of Arvon's energy – unless the completeness of it afforded him the mercurial capacity to go between, and to reconcile the apparently irreconcilable – meaning the anarchic Arvon *primum mobile* with the regulatory powers out there. Because that is what he did achieve: an established venture with which magic and the unaccountable could continue to do business, but which at the same time became, on the regulators' and public funders' terms, a model sustainable arts organisation.

Maybe there is something about the complete that carries its own metaphysics. So that the engagement of complete integrity will inform completely. Certainly there was the impression that David's integrity became the integrity of Arvon in its dealings with the world. And so much in evidence there was little else required to convince potential benefactors that Arvon was as good as his word.

A bit of a fanatic? He might have been if for a moment he'd wanted Arvon for himself. But component to his integrity was a wild-streak passion, real imagination, generosity reaching even beyond the generosity with which he gave Arvon open call on his time, and a Dionysian gift for good companionship. One needs to mention these if one hopes to explain the all-enabling sequence of working relationships he had with Arvon's Chairmen: Hal Hudson, Carol Hughes, Lawrence Sail, Brian Cox and Robin Chichester-Clark.

I should be careful not to trespass too far into the verifiable but I need to allow my coverage of Arvon's proto-magic to stretch this far. The contribution of each of these Chairmen was not simply unique – but appeared as the specific response to a critical imperative in Arvon's development. Each was remarkable, each made over to Arvon more of their time than they could conceivably have had to spare. Why Arvon should have been the serial recipient of such exact generosity ... well, if I've overplayed the word magic, my handle on metaphysics has come away in my hand. Of one thing though I do feel certain: whatever their contribution, it would have been largely ineffective, even inconceivable, without David's back-up, and without the sheer productive pleasure of working with him.

THE ARVON BOX

When David Pease retired he was given a box containing dedicated poems, messages, manuscripts, fragments and appreciations from some 150 of the 1,500 writers who by that time had worked for Arvon. The construction of the box was overseen by the Libanus Press, and I was detailed to collect it. Before I delivered it I took a peep inside. I felt I was hit by a kind of mage-wind – a gale of sunlight, chatter and back-chat and clear laughter. Not so much a memory-store as echoings of inescapable life. For me, just to think back on Arvon is to open such a box – a life gift which I can try but entirely fail to not take personally.

Except that mine, I find, is a two-tier box like a box of the expensive chocolates where the under-tier is entirely another adventure. Perhaps it's a constant in history that there are these two layers – the one comprised of macro-events that happen on the upper level in full collective glare and are component in an overall development; and then underneath, almost hidden, that of the micro-events, the day-to-day details that in sum are the grain to this unfolding life. If so then I guess that for the entire history to be living each layer must be unified by the lively register on an individual heart. As they are in my box. Here the two tiers, even though different, are bound together by the same eye for – I'm sorry, I'm going to say it again – magic.

The top tier contains the wide range of endowments (each warranting a section to itself in the verifiable history) that fell openly to Arvon and always out of the blue, and so would include:

The long term support of a scarcely believable number of exceptional, open-hearted writers (to test your credulity, take a look at Appendix 2).

The phenomenal chain of gifts and funding, and every link in that chain – each an amazement with the shock of an ambush (Appendix 3).

The response of grassroots Arvon to Janni Howker's absolute declaration that funding be found at once to secure Lumb Bank, then threatened with closure, as an Arvon Centre.

The efficient lunacy with which Kit, Sarah and Sophia Fraser corralled a large section of two nations into learning verse by heart as part of their Poetry Marathon. Which extraordinary event went a long way to funding their Moniack Mhor Arvon Centre in the Highlands.

Selima Hill, when she won the Arvon International Poetry Competition, shaking her head in a moment of disbelief before, in a simple reflex of heart, handing the cheque for £5,000 back as a gift to Arvon.

The spontaneous combustion that was the way the Friends of Arvon came suddenly into existence. Now getting on for one thousand members, and existing to foster the delight of writing and the encouragement of others. But also to support Arvon. The Friends' contributions have been constant, unqualified and of real significance.

The way that Nick Grant introduced Arvon to Duncan Lawrie Ltd, the private bank of which he was Chief Executive, so that Arvon benefited from not only his own endless guiding involvement, care and attention, but also the Bank's repeated sponsorship and support.

The on-and-on register of inspired fundraising events – the gala T.S. Eliot memorial reading at the Palace Theatre, the 1990 Savoy Literary Dinner where the artists donating their time included four of the country's leading chefs, Sotheby auctions, 'Arvon at the Races' – all of them, one way or another, underwritten by generosity: auctions of things donated; readings given by celebrated poets, writers and actors; and the organisation of each event the gift of someone's vision and exhaustive energy.

There's the through-good-times-and-bad support not always associated with public funding, led by the Arts Council and a line of Literature Directors, consistent with their engaged care and counsel.

Among the most recent, the blending of unquantifiable generosity and endeavour brought to fruition by the fiat of Helen Osbourne herself, and finally by Arvon's Chairman, Prue Skene and David Pease's successor, Helen Chaloner, with the opening of the John Osbourne Arvon Centre at The Hurst.

*   *   *

The jewelled memory store on the under-tier of the box is of another order. Since each person touched by Arvon has his or her own box, the selection in the under-space will be of her or his own memories – their own beads, their own thread. But each box is indispensable if the story is to be complete. Mine though has been so long overloaded it's broken open, and the memories all spilled around the floor. If you've time to share one or two, I'll reach for them at random.

*   *   *

Henry Williamson in a stormtrooper helmet, with a raven's feather in the bullet hole, arriving to read at the end of a course.

*   *   *

A student, a girl, maybe eighteen or nineteen. She arrives hunched, a knot of apprehension, the live ends sparking. She's watching each of us for a move, says 'But don't think I'm going to write anything.'

First day she finally does come to see us – last of all. Sits on the edge of her chair. We ask, 'Are you finding what you came for?'

Her eyes snatch at something. Then she's looking out of the window, then she draws the blind. We say gently, cautiously, 'Some people find it useful to have a theme to work with. This time we're suggesting The River.' Her eyes don't move, but maybe she did hear. She appears to be listening to something in the distance.

The second day we leave the students to themselves. In the evening she waits till I'm alone, then hands me a sheet of paper, carefully folded. She says, 'You're not to show it to anyone.' The poem is extraordinary. That once in a while when the gift is so much its own, so brittle and fine, it's best to keep well away.

The third day, again she turns up, my last appointment. I say, 'Your poem, so beautiful – there are a couple of things though.' I point to a phrase with my finger. She recoils as if I've put my hand on her knee. I smile. 'Don't worry,' I say, 'it's your poem.' 'I don't want anyone else seeing it,' she says. 'I don't want it read.'

The final day she arrives early. A new draft of the poem (which has taken account of my suggestion) and two other poems. I say, 'And you wouldn't think of reading these tonight, I mean sharing them?' She shakes her head. And then there is I think a smile. She says, 'You read them if you like. But you're not to say I wrote them.'

That evening, when the moment arrives, I unfold the poems, am taking a breath when she gets up from the sofa, walks across the room and takes them from me. And then she reads them, very quietly, but beautifully. When she's finished, no-one moves. Someone takes a deep breath. The girl isn't hunched any more. She appears to be taller.

*   *   *

At Totleigh Barton, a Starting to Write course. One of the students is the Mayor of Shaftesbury. 6′4″, ex-SAS, a sergeant I think, and the nation's Champion Town Crier. He's brought his bell with him. Mornings, 7.30 am reveille – from the lawn the clarion bell, and he cries his latest poem.

*   *   *

Fairfax, Michael Campbell-Cole (guitarist, racing-driver) and I are running a course for Children in Care – young people who've shoplifted, set fire to things, tried to top themselves – on the usual one condition: they must want to write. The impressive guy who is organising the course says he's taking a big risk: 'It's when they get bored they make trouble.' He sends a pantechnicon loaded with art materials, games, gym gear, canoes – aids to combat boredom. We lock them in the barn. There's no trouble on the course (less than on some school courses). Merely another Arvon course, unique, unforgettable.

The last day Fairfax and I are holding our final meetings. A lad, maybe sixteen, a lank with the hardened look of someone who's been sent down too often – but who's been fine to work with, and has made a couple of poems he's pleased with. Does he think he'll go on writing? He shrugs and nods at the same time. Does he have any plans? He says he'd like to go in the army but . . . 'But?' 'With what they got on me, they won't take me. More than likely.' No feeling in the voice, but beneath there is real feeling. I say, 'If it's any use, I'll write you a reference.' There's the flinch. For a moment Fairfax and I see the look of hurt, or grief. Then he's back together as if he hasn't heard. He looks away. Fairfax says, 'You heard that, did you, what John said?' 'Yes, but he didn't mean it.' Fairfax takes a pull, longer than usual, on his fag. Then he says, 'You say that, and the last three days we've been talking about poetry, and words, and telling it for real.'

After supper (the guy who organised the course has returned for the evening and is startled to find the young people quietly getting the washing up done before the final reading) in the barn the lad breaks into everyone's chatter, says he's found this poem he'd like to read. It's a poem by Thomas Hardy.

*   *   *

Totleigh Barton, four mementos:

At the foot of the Monk's Room stairs the heavy patterned blanket curtain – a gift from Antoinette's and my neighbour Granny Beer. 'That old thing? Get on, you take 'im!'

The dining room – in a niche in the wall there's the little handbell: a gift from Eric Walter White for summoning to supper.

Still in the sitting room last time I was there the gross, cherry-wood pipe with a bowl as big as your fist. I bought it in 1955 in Monte Carlo from the tobacconist at the top of the Casino square. It was when I was in Monaco, painting with Edmond Kapp. A year or so ago I dropped in on Totleigh as one of the Centre Directors was showing a couple of people around. When they came to the sitting room I'm afraid I was listening. 'And that,' she said, 'is Ted Hughes' pipe!'

Again in the dining room, Edmond Kapp's lithograph of that wonderful woman, Madame Eidenschenk-Patin, French delegate to the League of Nations. She's watched over the proceedings at table these thirty-two years. But no-one should get ideas – she's strictly on loan.

*   *   *

An Open Course at Lumb Bank. A difficult session with a woman who is showing me her radio play. I'm stuck . . .

structure, dialogue, the plot: I cannot come up with anything to say. It's hopeless, so maybe it's best to come clean. In the end I fudge it. I say, 'But try it on someone else. When it comes to drama I'm not sure I'm much use.'

In the middle of my next session the door's flung open. She's back, gleaming – like she's on the receiving end of the annunciation. 'You won't guess,' and I didn't, 'a phone-call, the BBC, my play, they've . . . they've taken it.' I did what I could, but I was feeling how my heart went out to the bloke in the poem, the one in the barber's queue who criticised how the white owl on the shelf had been stuffed – only to see it wink, and fly out the door.

* * *

The Naval Commander who at the outbreak of the course put a bottle of Teachers under Fairfax's pillow, put another under mine. A year later he sent each of us six volumes of his surprising poems, in large format, beautifully produced.

Then there was the Major, Indian Army, retired. Voice from before the War, from under his moustache, from the side of his mouth. Great favourite with the young women. A brief-case of poems, the poems he'd had in mind: England, seemly love, views of the garden – each mentioned in despatches. There wasn't a productive lot I could find to say about them or, I guess, that he wanted to hear. But there was one poem, to his wife, that seemed to have got away from him. 'I particularly like that one,' I said. 'Yes,' he said, 'good one. Sent what-sisname a copy, you know, the Laureate chap.' 'You mean . . . Ted Hughes?' I said. 'And did you hear from him?' 'Oh yes, long letter, nice chap.'

Or the Starting to Write course at Lumb Bank, supper the first evening, surveying the raw recruits, wondering: will I survive? And there mid-table the Countess of Stowe already and irretrievably in conversation with the Secretary of the Nottingham Miners' Union.

* * *

David Gascoyne, the visiting reader, in his panama hat umpiring the last afternoon cricket match, Fairfax's team against mine; and Judy, his wife, with a slog-sweep, a cow-shot, smashing a Fairfax dolly into the long grass and running . . . run after run after run.

* * *

Daunted? I'll say! She looks like the Ice Queen stepped from the pages of a fashion magazine I'd need to buy on instalments. She hands me a crisp manuscript: profiles of successful women. I read a bit, and then try reading somewhere else. You know when you drink something unbelievably cold, there's the pain you get, the freezing between the eyes. Finally I say quietly, 'Anything else you've written?' She's hesitating. Then she hands me these scruffy old few pages. I begin to read, and immediately am apart with what I'm reading . . . about the young brother, this living young brother she lost in his prime. 'Oh boy,' I whisper, 'so you can write.' When I look up someone else is there: a girl, gone soft, she looks Irish to me, and most of the mask seems to have melted, running down her face, with the tears.

* * *

Bill and Barbara Hughes, Lumb Bank Centre Directors, it's their doing – they get an Arvon posse of writers (which includes Michael Baldwin, Stan Barstow, Paddy Kitchen, Colin Spencer and, as our front man, Ted Hughes) invited to the HMI Annual

Conference in Malvern. We're allotted two days to introduce the Inspectors to the Arvon experience: get them writing, give some individual attention. It looks like it's being a great success. Yes, that's how it looks. Arvon on the brink of having persuaded the Establishment. At the end of the Conference, the Plenary Session. Ted Hughes is invited to sum up for Arvon. He suggests that maybe they now have an idea of what Arvon . . . and that's as far as he gets. A voice shrill with injury and indignation from near the back – a gainly young woman with the fatal aspect of the goddess Kali. 'Yes, I do have an idea, and I wouldn't allow my students within a mile of Arvon. Or of . . . that horrible little man!' By some magnetism our eyes are drawn . . . to the fifth row and the small figure in pilloried posture trying to make little of himself. No, of course I'm not naming him (and he's not one of those mentioned above). For a time Ted is standing there, like an epic hero surveying the ruins of illusion's bright citadel. At last he breaks that silence of no return – and anyone who ever heard him speak will know the sound as he says, 'What a very unlucky thing!'

* * *

No forgetting Jonathan, Icarus of the Paris bourse, come with 800 computer-struck poems and a militant disinterest in learning to write. And in cooking. He persuaded his team to let him ring Fortnum & Mason and have them despatch a vast Glynbourne-style picnic hamper. Who were we to complain? We'd sampled the poems, so now spare us the cooking. But with Totleigh Barton being out of the way, and the weather being hot, the hamper's contents on arrival were rancid. But not the all-forgiving Methuselah of bubbly which, should you need to prove the story, still graces the ledge above the Totleigh Barton front stairs.

* * *

Our dear Mary Dups. Gone seventy, I'd guess. A stroke had left the best part of her speech and her right side impaired. She was heavy and tall, walked with a stick unsafely, her bulk unstable in a kind of long kaftan. On the same course were the five lads from a Gravesend comprehensive – a boys' gang with its cloudless solidarity, and at least two gifted writers. They watched Mary Dups sidelong – social barrier, barrier of age, plus the fair bet she's gone gaga – they kept out of her way.

To focus imagination, we had a 'catch-all' theme for the course: The Revenant. The last evening Mary touched my shoulder with the rubber end to her stick: when the students all read, I was to read her piece, 'The Counting Garden'. It had come to her the first evening outside – the late August stillness, the pigeon purring in the chestnut tree, a flight of mallards down to the river . . . and she's back in Suffolk, the summer of '44, at dawn, out from all night in the control room, stood on the lawn, listening for the Skylarks, her boys, her Canadian flyers, to make it down from the clouds, stuttering home. The ones that did make it. All those that didn't . . . Curly, Johnnie, and Crookie the squadron's leader, last seen going down 'in a swirling pillar of fire'. And she the one left to bicycle over and, with the Padre, tell it to his little wife, and their gurgling baby. Ending the piece with:

In the silent mess, breakfast tables laid for 40. The Cook Sergeant says, 'Plenty of bacon for all,' the tears falling black on her blue shirt.

My companions, my lovely friends, who on the edge of eternity asked for a token of affection. Why was I not taught more of the sadness of war, and the joy of generosity – but left lost in the mores of Victorian morality? It would have been something in the summer dawn, and have mattered not one bit now.

The song of skylarks and the scent of Je Reviens still
break my ageing heart.

Somehow I made it to the end, my voice more or less steady.
After a little I looked up into the silence. Mary smiled at me, and
nodded. But what chiefly I remember are the faces of the five
lads. Each appeared empty and to be staring into emptiness, as if
waiting for what was bound in the end to dawn on him.

*   *   *

Steve and Josie were the Centre Directors. Josie was a north
country maid who displaced the mind of just about every
wandering mower who came to Totleigh Barton. In addi-
tion she adorned Totleigh with flowers and a range of productive animals, including an omnivoracious goat, and a
bantam rooster with an ambition to impose himself on the
universe.

Kathleen Raine came to read on the final night of
Fairfax's and my course. Next morning I was in the garden,
looking at the sky and breathing away the whispers of hang-
over, when I was struck on the shin by a meteorite. I howled
and looked down and there three feet from me, neck
extended, the venom-spit eyes of a basilisk, was Josie's
rooster. I drew my foot back slowly and then . . . the rooster
was airborn, tumbling in a disarray of wings and tail feath-
ers down the sky. I imagine the seraphic smile settling on my
countenance when . . . 'John!' came the voice from Heaven.
I turned. There at the end of the path stood Kathleen in
wrathful aspect.

'But Kathleen,' I whimpered, 'he hit me first'.

'That doesn't matter,' she said. 'You're bigger than he is.'

*   *   *

On one of the first Totleigh Barton courses an unknown
student wrote:

> Covered wagon
> Thatched into the land
> Stitched up with time
> Earthen walls white
> Washed with mud
> Straw cracks in the wind.
>
> Behind our earthwork –
> Moated by mudded streams
> And growth of briar
> And barb and nettle – we weave
> Until gold gleams
> The thread of our lives.

A LAST THOUGHT

The other night Fairfax and I were back on our bench in The Bull, getting on with the conversation. We started wondering, would we, restored to relative youth and with providence in identical attendance, have any chance in today's context of allowing Arvon to stumble to its feet? After all, what's so different? The courses are just as alive, productive and individually valued as ever. So surely it would have to be possible. For someone maybe but not, we decided, for us. That time (it was the 1960s, don't forget) was unique; possibility was abroad, a wave-band able to carry even our programme.

Fairfax was looking thoughtfully at where Bob's Chair was gone from the end of the bar. 'The world has moved on,' he said, but not with a great deal of concern.

Moved on! In Arvon's early days it had been pens and notebooks and a queue for one of the two typewriters (there was also a queue for the loo, but back then no-one complained). Had laptops even been thought of? If so you'd have needed a mobile Albert Hall to house the circuitry for what's operational today in one slim laptop. Today a student is as likely to have a laptop as a toothbrush.

And then imagine how far we'd get now if we suggested taking fifteen youngsters, boys and girls, out into the sticks for five days to write poems – just the two of us and no supervision. How far? The local slammer. Actually I'm wrong, because we'd be lost on the way: the paperwork, the application questionnaires, the evaluation forms . . . and then the parent groups, insurance companies, fire officers, health and safety inspectors. No, we'd have been a couple of wasps in a jam jar: all buzz, no sting.

'So there's the problem,' says I. 'Do you want civil liberties?

Or to protect society from terrorists?'

'Terrorists?'

'Yes, the Baader-Meinhof, remember?'

We mused on this for a while.

'Anything we should have done differently?'

'You suggesting we had any choice?'

There was one thing I'd been wondering about recently . . . but we were now too deep into the evening for me to get my mind round it. But I have wondered some more since. As one can see from the Annual Report and Accounts 1972–73 (Appendix 1), the Open Course Programme (courses open to any member of the public) was a relatively late development. Simply because at the outset we hadn't the means to promote it. Once in place it began, word of mouth, to promote itself. As the response grew, so emphasis on the Open Courses increased. Not surprisingly because Arvon was suddenly into Earned Income, which not only served to impress potential funders, but could be seen as a basis for survival. At the same time the country's education policy, with its increasing curriculum demands, was making it more and more difficult for teachers, teacher trainees and schools to find time for Arvon courses.

An Arvon fundamentalist might claim that an Arvon course by any other name is an Arvon course – and with justification because it seems so clear that the spirit of Arvon, as expressed by the commitment, excitement, fulfilment of tutors and students, is constant. And yet it is a view that fails to recognise a core division. How does one explain it? Take Arvon's adopted superscription, 'The fire in the flint shows not till it be struck'. At the outset it seemed taken as read by everyone involved with Arvon that the fire this referred to was that of the individual's imagination – and that the key to its unlocking was an act of genuine education. The fire was, in other words, universally and individually of transforming and formative power.

But with the Open Course programme becoming the main focus of activity, and increasingly the means of survival, a new realism saw to it that the organisation became more responsive to the market place. Seemingly the courses were essentially the same, but there was a new emphasis which, if one chooses to see it this way, infected even the definition of the fire in the flint. If the market place is now relevant, achievement becomes part of the business. Those paying a market price for their course are likely to want something marketable to show for it. Suddenly platform, profile, publication, success and even celebrity have been insinuated into the value system. If they help fill the courses, and thereby contribute to survival, the organisation must take account of them. This new market sense may even influence the choice of tutors, and in subtle ways the slant, content and structure of the course. So now the fire to be struck necessarily includes the desire and ability to succeed in the market place.

No-one's implying that Arvon should claim some phoney high ground and view wealth creation or individual success with contempt. But what may be important is that it realise that here are two forces that, following their own interests, will tend to move in counter directions. If Arvon is conscious of this, then it will be in a position to determine which direction to follow – or whether the two can be reconciled. Which of course they can – because wherever the needs of any two create between them impasse there is always the way through via an overview of unity. All courses are educational. Genuine life, cradle to grave, is self-expressive, is creative, is guided by imagination, is education. Any other so-called life is truancy.[1]

Late as it was I was perhaps somewhere alive to this thought because at the end of some smokey silence I said to

---

1. Amit Goswami, in his book *The Self-aware Universe*, demonstrates how from the viewpoint of quantum physics individual creativity and a meaningful universe predicate each other.

Fairfax, 'The flaw in the stone – unseen till the stone comes in two. Know what was the worst moment for me in all our time with Arvon?'

'You're about to tell me,' he said.

To mark Totleigh Barton being finally entrusted to Arvon, we'd had a marvellous young letter-cutter, Sebastian Brook, carve a line from John Donne's 'The Good Morrow' into a massive rough slate we'd unearthed from a neighbouring shippon. 'Whatever dyes was not mixt equally.' Fairfax and I happened to be at Totleigh Barton soon after the slate with its rough-hewn italic inscription was delivered – it's only too clear why I might have wanted to share again with him what happened next. But it's the say-so of my Irish grandmothers, and their grasp of the unlucky, that has me, for everyone's sake, leave it here in the open. As the pair of us gently lowered the slate on to the grass it unaccountably and quite silently fell apart. The stone came in two. So effortless it was for a moment as if the spell that bound the earth had been lifted. We looked at each other, and saw how the other was listening.

It was next morning we contacted Mr Morris, a monumental mason in Bideford. He said, 'You're in luck, I'm due out Sheepwash today.' He fetched the slate, fixed it back together with a German stone-glue, and held it bound and immovable in a steel frame. So now it's there on the wall. If the fault has shown itself and is healed, the stone is more dependable.

When I'd recalled all this Fairfax nodded, and then drank some beer. And then quite suddenly across the table, he held out his hand. I took it. And we were laughing.

More laughter! Writing all this I've sometimes worried my treatment makes light of the commitment of so many people. And yet it has been the lightness that has tempered Arvon, and kept it radical, deep-rooted – William Blake's lightness of heart that 'kisses the joy as it flies'. A life force, and one that can champion life against the scrutinising caution, the dead-hand circumspection and joylessness that all but creative bureaucracy seems always to impose on its operations and its clients – those that fall under its spell.

W.B. Yeats wrote, 'Only when we are gay [and I take him to mean light-hearted] over a thing, and can play with it, do we show ourselves its master, and have minds clear enough for strength.' So as I see it light-heartedness is Arvon's strength. More than anything else it has characterised and sustained Arvon. It is what people who attend Arvon courses are, above all, touched by, and take away with them in the way of determination. It is what illuminates a successful course. It has power to fortify the spirit and the individual imagination – as is seen time and again in the strengthened resolve and restored enthusiasm of teachers returning to work in the classroom. It endures as the distinguishing feature of the Friends of Arvon; and part of their gift to Arvon is that they continually mirror this reality back to the frontline operation. It is the sound, like universal laughter, one hears when one lifts the lid on the Arvon Box.

After a recent course, a student wrote, 'One of the exceptional aspects of the week was the freedom of pressure to produce anything of a particular kind – the sense that devotion to the process of writing, whatever that might be, was what mattered – but all the time a spirit of delight, a sort of mercurial mischief, ran through it all.'

So he got in on it, did he? Mercury. But of course, the patron of thieves – not the thieves who mug old ladies but those who nick eternity's property and bring it to earth. Mischievous, reckless, unaccountable – attributes of Hermes, who has wings on his (or her!) trickster's sandals, and the gift to thermal to the gods, hover over the world of we mortals, or plummet to the place of shades. Light-heartedness is serious business. Hermes, the most reliable type of the Imagination. Hermes, the Guide of Souls. Not some souls, all souls.

That's why Arvon's door is open. And anyone looking to come in but lacking the means, Arvon will give them a bursary. Look at the list of writers (Appendix 2) who've come to teach . . . call that lot exclusive? Or the long list of students who've gone on to successful writing careers?

The landlord called time – confirming that in The Bull too, the world had moved on. Fairfax stubbed out . . . no, not his last fag.

'Okay,' he said, 'so let's end it with the best moment.'

'The best moment?' I closed my eyes, rocked backwards and forwards trying to think. Then it came to me out of the dark.

'When we read the first independent evaluation. From the Crediton Three, the D-Stream Baader-Mienhof: "We had been called on to write as if writing mattered . . . I think what was shattering was that suddenly everything mattered".'

And to that Fairfax and I drained our glasses.

APPENDIX I:
ANNUAL REPORT AND ACCOUNTS
1972–73

Appendix 1

<u>FOREWORD</u>

The living success of any year for Arvon is exactly measured
by the success of its courses; and so the detailed report is the
true account.   This however must be given its context, and much
of 1972-73 was a time of lingering difficulties making impossible
any final assessment of progress in the establishment of Arvon.

It was the Foundations first full year with a professional
Administrator, and for the first two thirds of it he found himself
operating in a situation of unsettling insecurity.   This was
brought about in part by the shaky finances, and in part by the
persistent delays in final registration of company and charity.
We should congratulate Peter Mason on the way he saw Arvon through
a very difficult time.   By the end of the year, however, the financial
pressure was, in the short term at least, relieved.   On the first of
April 1973 Arvon Foundation Limited, a charity, was officially constituted.

Apart from the increase of capital knowledge that comes with each
course (and 1972 saw one unsuccessful course --- from which a great
deal was learned!) the main profit of the year lay in the successful
experiment with three new types of courses (Music, Teachers, and Drama -
see separate reports).

Perhaps the main difficulty that has not so much emerged as been
confirmed in the last year is the problem of bringing unlimited seemingly committed enthusiasm on the part of Educational Authorities and
establishments to fulfilment, and more astonishing of sustaining, even
after enthusiastic reception of a course, excitement from one year to
the next.   However, even so the bookings for 1973-74 currently look
encouraging, and we hope to more than meet our aim of conducting 24
courses within the year.

Clearly the proposed Northern development at Lumb Bank, Ted Hughes'
house in Yorkshire, dominates the future.   If this goes ahead, and
currently the prospect is promising, it will clearly be a major development, transforming the status of Arvon from regional to national.

<u>COURSES 1972 - 1973</u>

4th - 9th April 72	13 students from the Somerset Local Education Authority Area. Tutored by D.M. THOMAS and JENI COUZYN with CHARLES CAUSLEY as visiting reader. This course produced quite a lot of poetry of a high standard.
16th - 21st April	13 students from La Sainte Union College, Southampton. Tutored by MICHAEL BALDWIN and JOHN FAIRFAX with JOHN MOAT as visiting reader. The course was highly successful with a considerable amount of good work being written by the students.
21st - 26th April	13 students from Culham College, Abingdon. JON STALLWORTHY and IAN HAMILTON as tutors with PHILLIP CALLOW as reader. There was a core of students on this course who had come for the wrong reasons. As neither of the tutors had worked for us before and we had a new Course Manager there was some difficulty in breaking down the barriers, but I think that in the end something was achieved.

COURSES 1972 - 1973 (CONTINUED)

23rd - 25th June

3 students from Culham College, Abingdon. KIT BARKER and JOHN FAIRFAX as tutors. In contrast to the last course, despite the poor attendance this course was extremely valuable.

2nd - 6th July

14 students from Rolle College, Exmouth, tutored by JOHN MOAT and JOHN FAIRFAX with RONALD DUNCAN as visiting reader. These courses for students from the English Department of Rolle College have now become a regular feature of our programme and are always highly successful.

30th July - 4th August

13 school children from the Hampshire Local Education Authority area. Tutored by ALAN BROWNJOHN and PETER REDGROVE with CHARLES CAUSLEY as visiting reader. The tutors were very impressed by the hard work and general attitude of the children. The standard of their work improved a great deal during the course.

6th - 11th August

Drama Course - see separate report, "The Playwright in Education".

27th August - 1st Sept

Open Course - 11 students from very mixed backgrounds and covering a very wide age range. This course was something of an experiment, but the group gelled together well and the students got a lot out of it. Tutored by HOWARD SERGEANT, PAUL ROCHE and HILARY CORKE, with DAVID HOLBROOK as the visiting reader.

1st - 3rd September

6 young writers invited to Totleigh at the time of the AGM to further their interest in poetry. Given further help during the weekend by JOHN FAIRFAX, they also received an address from ROBERT GATHORNE-HARDY on the Sunday morning.

2nd - 4th February 73

In-Service Teachers Course - see separate report.

6th - 11th March

Music Course - see separate report.

16th March

Poetry Day for local schools attended by 33 children and conducted by VERNON SCANNELL and DAVID HARSENT. A highly stimulating introduction to Poetry, the Arvon Foundation, and Totleigh Barton Manor, that we hope will become a regular feature of our programme.

THE PLAYWRIGHT IN EDUCATION

The Arvon Foundation decided to extend its work this year to include Drama. It was thought that a valid contribution to Drama Education and one which was in keeping with the aims of the Foundation would be to involve the Playwright himself. He is seldom involved in Education - only his scripts are used.

As soon as we get away from Poetry, around which Arvon's work has centred so far, we encounter the problems of the involvement of the interpretive as well as the creative artist. The Playwright is only one part of the creative process that involves directors, designers, actors and audience.

Appendix 1

We obviously couldn't involve all these groups in our courses and
having decided to use the Playwright as the central figure in our
Drama work, we decided to use the Director to represent the other
groups.

The first course organised along these lines took place at
TOTLEIGH BARTON MANOR from the 1st - 4th August 1972, tutored by
TIM APPLEBEE, Assistant Director at the Northcott Theatre, Exeter;
and the Playwright, DAVID CREGAN, one of the Royal Court group of
writers. The students were mainly Secondary School children from
various parts of Devon.

Both tutors were very experienced in improvisation and studio
work and a considerable amount of time was spent in this kind of
work. During the course the students were able to experience a
wide variety of stimulating studio work, improvisation, word games,
and movement in a relaxed atmosphere. This built up over the five
days into what can only be described as a happening at the end of
the course, spontaneously devised by the group, and fully justifying
the direction the work had taken. The students were also able to
find out a great deal about Playwrighting and the Theatre in the
informal discussions with the tutors. Both tutors were very excited
about the potentialities of the renovated barn at Totleigh as a working area for drama. They found in it similar qualities to those
which have excited the poets that have used Totleigh Barton Manor
and were able to draw on these qualities in their work. None of
the students wrote anything during the course but we would hope that
the stimulation of working and living in an informal and congenial
atmosphere for five days with professional theatre people might have
helped them in their understanding of drama and creativity.

We hope that in the future our drama work will build on the
success of this first course. Whilst we would always hope that our
Drama Courses do not get bogged down in the literary side of playwrighting, we would also hope to provide students with an opportunity
during the course of writing. We think that there would be a lot to
be gained by the students writing, for example, either individually
or in groups, a page of dialogue, and then having the opportunity of
seeing how it works when produced and amending it accordingly. Here
the group would be making full use of the tutors. The first stage
of word games and improvisation taken by the Director and Playwright
stimulating the group into stage two - writing, help and advice, where
wanted, being given by the Playwright. The script could then be
produced by the Director using other members of the group as actors.
From seeing it produced, and hearing the comments of the Director,
Playwright, and the others, the writer could then amend the script
and so the process could develop.

IN SERVICE TEACHERS COURSE

A weekend course for eleven teachers from Devon, Cornwall and
Hampshire, was held at Totleigh Barton Manor, from 2nd - 4th February.
The course was tutored by John Fairfax and John Moat.

The course had two main aims:

    (i) to acquaint teachers with Arvon's work and aims - and
        that in a way impossible by circular or report, namely
        by giving them the opportunity to experience both the
        freedom and the precision of Arvon's methods in the
        surroundings which have been specifically established
        for the work; and to afford them the opportunity of
        tasting themselves something of the excitement and
        intensity of a full Arvon course.

IN SERVICE TEACHERS COURSE (CONTINUED)

(ii) to discuss with teachers ways in which the Centre and
its activities can best serve the educational system,
and how it can be utilized to achieve maximum benefit
to both them and their pupils in the routine situation
of the classroom.

The following is from a report on the course by D. Kessel B.A.,
F.R.G.S., Head of English at Romsey School, Hampshire, one of the
teachers on the course:

"I attended the course, a little perplexed about what to expect
and what the ultimate benefit might be. I found the major
benefit was that it makes one more aware of the process of
creativity, which, in either written work, or criticism of
literature, is a fundemental factor in English teaching. The
course cannot be expected to offer any set formula, but, in
stimulating conditions, enables one to see the whole process
from both the professionals' and pupils' viewpoints, and
encourages teachers to explore its possibilities.

I think that all teachers on my course realised the value of
the atmosphere at Arvon. Relaxing, less inhibiting, it encourages
creativity, building its own momentum. Do we spend enough
thought in school, on providing the correct situation and
atmosphere? Can some of the factors at Arvon, which helped
our own creativity, be applied with benefit to the school
situation? School time-tables cut short work in progress,
juxtapose unsuitable lessons before or after English, may
force a class into an unsuitable room. Secondary schools
possess many specialist rooms - what does English merit?

How does a practical course, such as at Arvon, compare with
a series of lectures? Lectures can efficiently make teachers
aware of developments in English. However, creativity, which
is increasingly one factor in the English teachers' skills,
can best be appreciated on a practical course, especially one
where teachers can meet professional writers. I am sure that
many teachers find it difficult to inspire and guide children
in their own writing, to discuss the childrens' or modern
writers' work. Many people are also questioning the looseness
of previous 'creative writing'.

English has begun to see the unity of its subject again.
Literature is central to this work, and arvon could give teachers
a chance to experiment. This aspect of the course could profitably
be developed, with more practical work and visiting speakers,
although the very informal nature of the course should be retained.

For me, the main value of the course was that it opened up the
possibility of doing something which Education must develop in
the future; to run out-of-school courses. A school group could
benefit enourmously from a course such as Arvon runs for young
people, designing it as part of the school curiculum."

The following is from a report by the tutors:

"Initially we were a little nervous that the teachers might be
suspicious of and even hostile towards what we were attempting
to achieve. We needn't have been. The group responded with
excitment, and what, frankly, was impressive open-mindedness.

Appendix 1

At the end of the weekend all the teachers said that they
had found the time a real break and refreshment; they said
that they valued the 'tutorials' with the poets, and that
they felt they would have a new confidence in the classroom
in discussing the problems and the merits of creative work.
They had been impressed by the atmosphere of the place, had
seen how conducive it was to imaginative work; and they
valued the informality which had enabled them to make contact
with one another and to discuss at a remove from 'the workshop'
the problems and theories of their own profession. Without
exception they were eager to implicate their pupils in Arvon's
activities.

For our part, we enjoyed the course immeasurably, and found
our discussion with the teachers invaluable in our assessment
of, and approach to, the Foundation's work."

MUSIC COURSE

A music course was held at Totleigh Barton Manor from 6th to
11th March 1973. This course was attended by eleven students from
the Music Department of Filton Technical College, Bristol, and their
Lecturer in Charge. It was tutored by MALCOLM WILLIAMSON and TIM
PORTER.

The following is from a report by Malcolm Williamson on the course:

"It was splendid to be able to be free to work with students in
the way I chose.

We chose to create an opera, as something beyond the capacity of
the students but worth the attempt; and with the benign help of
their tutor we succeeded beyond what I could have dreamed possible.
Saturday afternoon saw a complete performance of a valid opera
with orchestra, staging, solo singing and ensemble singing. Every
student participated in the performance; each had written words
and music to a scene, had orchestrated it, copied the orchestra
parts, rehearsed it with his peers.

This was a seemingly incredible feat, particularly in four days;
and it was possible only because of the flexibility of the
Foundation which made it all possible. I was impressed with the
way in which the students' creative stamina increased daily, and
in the end each had a creation (in most cases his/her first) to
take away and cherish."

The following is from a report by B. Snary, Lecturer-in-Charge of
the Music Section of the Department of Music, Art & Drama at Filton
Technical College, who attended the course:

"Words cannot explain fully what each member feels about the visit,
but many tears were shed, both visibly and invisibly by male and
female alike, when Malcolm had to leave early because of the train
strike. Such was the overwhelming emotional experience that each
person went through - an experience which no student will surely
ever forget.

What was achieved? An opera, 'Cinderella', was conceived, libretto
written, music composed and orchestrated for 9 instruments, parts
copied out, five vocal soloists and orchestra rehearsed, and the
whole performed, in four days!

Appendix 1

The opera was in three acts, with four scenes in each act.
Each individual was entirely responsible for one scene. This
shows the amount of work covered by the twelve who went on
the course. Malcolm Williamson inspired us all to compose
music of which many people did not realise they were capable.
No student has ever worked harder and the lack of any financial
assistance for the students showed their considerable enthusiasm
for the course which itself amply repaid them with a never-to-be
forgotten musical experience".

The following are some comments by the students written on their
return to College:

"The course provided an opportunity to forget about the problems
of everyday living and concentrate on music: This together with
the splendid atmosphere of the house and countryside helped everyone to create something not only as an individual but as a member
of the group".

"I have never experienced such willingness to work into the early
hours of the morning. Both Tim and Malcolm encouraged us in
every possible way, which made us determined to keep up this
unbelievable pace. Leaving was one of the greatest disappointments
I have experienced. I feel triumphant, yet sad. I feel I really
achieved something".

"One of the most useful facts was that the tools I required were
close at hand: I could immediately contact any of the musicians.
It was good to know that the piece I wrote was actually going to
be performed".

"One of the more unfortunate facts of life of a college such as ours
is that what compositional work we do has to be done in isolation.
The Arvon Course gave us the opportunity not only to devote ourselves entirely to our own composition, but also to hear and
participate directly in each others' composition. Under the
inspired guidance of Malcolm and Tim, a very real and intense
group feeling was created, born musically and emotionally, which
affected us all. It is particularly satisying to know, we can
share the experience since we have been able to produce a work
containing music which for some of us represents our greatest
achievement to date. I am sure that by giving us the chance to
work with each other and with two great musicians the course has
brought each of us to a better understanding of our own musicianship".

DATA

1. Twenty five artists have been involved with our work this year,
    fourteen of them (those marked with an asterisk) for the first time:

*	Tim Applebee	*	David Harsent
	Michael Baldwin	*	David Holbrook
	Kit Barker		Ted Hughes
*	Alan Brownjohn		John Moat
*	Phillip Callow	*	Tim Porter
	Charles Causley		Paul Roche
*	Hilary Corke		Peter Redgrove
*	Jeni Couzyn	*	Vernon Scannell
*	David Cregan	*	Howard Sergeant
	Ronald Duncan	*	Jon Stallworthy
	John Fairfax		D. M. Thomas
*	Ian Hamilton	*	Malcolm Williamson
	Robert Gathorne-Hardy		

Appendix 1

2.		71/72	72/73
Number of students attending Arvon Foundation courses		93	150
Number of students attending courses organised by outside groups		-	74
TOTAL number of students using Totleigh Barton Manor		93	224

3. Geographical breakdown of attendances:

Number of students attending Arvon Foundation Courses:

From South Western Arts Association area:

Devon	71
Cornwall	3
Somerset	15
Dorset	1
Gloucestershire	12
	102

From Southern Arts Association area:

Hampshire	28
Berkshire	20
	48

BALANCE SHEET AT 31ST MARCH 1973

		£	1972
GENERAL FUND:			
As at 1st April 1972		-	53
Add: Estimated value of Books and Records donated during year		100	-
		100	53
Less: Deficiency for year transferred from Income and Expenditure Account		573	(53)
DEFICIT		£473	NIL
Represented by:-			
FIXED ASSETS - Per Schedule		352	
CURRENT ASSETS:			
Stock	23		
Payments in Advance	162		
Cash in Hand	37		
	222		
LESS: CURRENT LIABILITIES:			
Creditors and Accrued Expenses	362		
Course fees received in advance	343		
Bank Overdraft	342		
	1,047		
NET CURRENT LIABILITIES:		825	
EXCESS LIABILITIES:		£473	NIL

We have examined the above Balance Sheet and attached Income and Expenditure and Revenue Accounts for the year and certify that they are in accordance with the records, information and explanations supplied to us.

24, Southernhay East,
EXETER,
Devon.

PEPLOW, WARREN & FURLER.

Chartered Accountants

9th August, 1973
VCT/RLW/RS

Appendix I

THE ARVON FOUNDATION

INCOME AND EXPENDITURE ACCOUNT FOR THE YEAR ENDED 31ST MARCH 1973

			£	1972
INCOME:-	from Courses		1,019	725
	from Letting		185	-
			1,204	725
Less:	Course Expenditure:-			
	Tutors and Readers Fees	1,084		
	Tutors and Readers Expenses	121		
	Course Managers' fees	145		
	Provisions	387		
	Laundry	100		
	Miscellaneous	61		
			1,898	1,225
NET COST OF COURSES			694	500
Add:	Administration Expenditure			
	Administration salaries and wages	1,614		1,471
	Literary Advisers' Fees	300		-
	Motor Expenses, Travelling and Subsistence	474		104
	Printing, Postage and Stationery	220		47
	Telephone	100		160
	Light and Heat	165		127
	Rates	54		46
	Insurance	193		199
	Repairs and Maintenance	30		8
	Cleaning and Gardening	61		41
	Right of Way payment	100		100
	Bank Charges	10		13
	Accountancy Fees	35		-
	Applicants' Expenses	-		68
	Bursary:- G. Casale	500		-
	Sundries	39		327
	Depreciation: Motor Vehicle	20		
	Equipment	22		
			3,937	2,711
COST OF COURSES AND ADMINISTRATION			£4,631	£3,211

THE ARVON FOUNDATION

SCHEDULE OF FIXED ASSETS AT 31ST MARCH 1973

		£	
MOTOR VEHICLES:			
Ford Thames 15 cwt Van - at cost	40		
Less: Depreciation for the Year	20		
		20	
EQUIPMENT:			
Imperial Typewriter - at cost	51		
Duplicator - at cost	83		
Tape Recorder - at cost	103		
Fire Extinguisher - at cost	17		
	254		
Less: Depreciation for the year	22		
		232	
BOOKS at valuation		40	
RECORDS at valuation		60	
		£352	

APPENDIX 2:
WRITERS WHO HAVE WORKED FOR ARVON

Paul Ableman
Paul Abbott
Dannie Abse
John Abulafia
Juliet Ace
Kathy Acker
Roger Ackling
Anna Adams
Sally Adams
Fleur Adcock
Dhiran Adebayo
John Agard
Patience Agbabi
Allan Ahlberg
Rukhsana Ahmad
Tim Albery
Vivien Alcock
Elizabeth Alexander
Lynne Alexander
Roger Allam
Foz Allan
Benedict Allen
Judy Allen
David Allison
Gillian Allnutt
David Almond
Moniza Alvi
Alba Ambert
Stephen Amidon
Jo Anderson
Linda Anderson
Moira Andrew
Roselle Angwin
Joan Anim-Addo
Tim Applebee
John Arden
Cindy Ariste
Aileen Armitage
Simon Armitage

Frankie Armstrong
Jake Arnott
Bill Ash
John Ash
Sue Ashby
Michael Ashe
Brad Ashton
David Ashton
Neil Astley
Donald Atkinson
Jeremy Attiyah
Liane Aukin
Leo Aylen
Trezza Azzopardi

Andrea Badenoch
Jane Bailey
Paul Bailey
Peter Bain
Beryl Bainbridge
Elizabeth Baines
Rajeev Balasubra-
    manyam
Michael Baldwin
Sophie Balhetchet
Biyi Bandele-Thomas
Iain Banks
John Banville
Dulan Barber
A.L. Barker
Clive Barker
Elspeth Barker
George Barker
Howard Barker
Kit Barker
Nicola Barker
Pat Barker
Raffaella Barker
Sebastian Barker

Nick Barlay
Robert Barnard
Bruce Barnes
John Barrie
Patricia Barrie
Judith Barrington
Stan Barstow
Elizabeth Bartlett
Paul Bhattacharjee
Nina Bawden
Martin Bax
Gill Beadle
Adrian Beam
Richard Bean
Alan Beard
Francesca Beard
Richard Beard
Simon Beaufoy
Martyn Bedford
Viv Beeby
Patricia Beer
Jane Beeson
Dominic Behan
Rosalind Belben
Julia Bell
Shirley Bell
Stephen Benatar
David Benedictus
Ronan Bennett
Gerard Benson
Judy Benson
Peter Benson
Barbara Bentley
Asa Benveniste
Anne Beresford
Barry Bermange
Chaim Bermant
Elizabeth Berridge
James Berry

Maurice Bessman
Nicholas Best
Sujata Bhatt
Stephen Bill
Kate Bingham
John Binias
Dea Birkett
John Birtwhistle
Julia Blackburn
Thomas Blackburn
Terence Blacker
Malorie Blackman
John Blackmore
Ken Blakeson
Alan Bleasdale
Peter Blegvad
Nicholas Blincoe
Edward Blishen
Valerie Bloom
Tony Blundell
Steven Blyth
Ronald Blythe
Sam Boardman Jacobs
Eavan Boland
Alan Bold
G.A. Bond
Malika Booker
Martin Booth
Anne Born
John Bowen
Peter Bowker
Clare Boylan
Charles Boyle
Daniel Boyle
Jocelyn Boxall
Malcolm Bradbury
Jane Bradish-Ellames
Alfred Bradley
Celia Brayfield
Ian Breakwell
Jean 'Binta' Breeze
Lynn Breeze
John Brennan
Theresa Breslin
Simon Brett
Mark Brickman

Pam Brighton
Clive Brill
Joanna Briscoe
Edwin Brock
Jeremy Brock
Ansel Broderick
Alan Brooks
Roger Brooks
Pip Broughton
Andy Brown
Gary Brown
Jacqueline Brown
Molly Brown
Anthony Browne
Stuart Browne
Alan Brownjohn
Sandy Brownjohn
Sylvia Brownrigg
Jill Bruce
John Brunner
Judith Bryan
Louise Bryan
Lynne Bryan
Colette Bryce
Elizabeth Buchan
Tom Buchan
Paul Buck
Will Buckley
Peter Buckman
Basil Bunting
Anna Burns
Christopher Burns
Jim Burns
John Burnside
John Burrows
Simon Burt
Betty Burton
Duncan Bush
Ron Butlin
Catherine Byron

Alexandra Cadell
Simon Calder
Philip Callow
Stephanie Calman
Richard Cameron

Shirley Cameron
Andy Campbell
David Campbell
Katie Campbell
Ramsay Campbell
Michael Campbell-
  Cole
Graham Carey
Jennifer Carey
Maurice Carpenter
J.L. Carr
Angela Carter
Sydney Carter
Ciaran Carson
Michael Carson
Jim Cartwright
Jules Cashford
Nina Cassian
Annie Casteldine
Annie Caulfield
Charles Causley
David Caute
Russell Celyn-Jones
Aiden Chambers
Harry Chambers
Steve Chambers
Michael Chaplin
Sid Chaplin
Eric Chappell
Debjani Chatterjee
Amit Chaudhuri
Mavis Cheek
Joyce Cheeseman
Lisa Chermin
Anne Chisholm
Rosalyn Chissick
George Chorlton
Annie Christie
Caryl Churchill
Donald Churchill
Kate Clanchy
Anthony Clark
Brian Clark
Leonard Clark
Candida Clark
Thomas A. Clark

Gillian Clarke
Lindsay Clarke
Anthony Clavane
Brendan Cleary
Jo Clegg
Carol Clewlow
Tony Cliff
Marvin Close
Anne Cluysenaar
Bob Cobbing
Liza Cody
Jonathan Coe
Mandy Coe
Lin Coghlan
Barry Cole
Gladys Mary Coles
Jenny Colgan
Graham Collier
Barry Collins
Ian Collins
Merle Collins
Stewart Conn
Shane Connaughton
Cressida Connolly
Tony Connor
David Constantine
Dominic Cooper
Mary Cooper
William Cooper
David Cook
Stanley Cook
Judy Cooke
Wendy Cope
Paul Copley
Julia Copus
Judy Corbalis
Victoria Coren
Hilary Corke
Charlotte Cory
John Cotton
Frank Cottrell Boyce
Jeni Couzyn
Andrew Cowan
James Cowan
Paul Cowlan
Kerry Crabbe

Jim Crace
David Craig
Robert Crawford
David Cregan
Helen Cresswell
Iain Crichton Smith
Gillian Cross
Susan Crosland
Kevin Crossley-
   Holland
Anna Crowe
Barry Cryer
Allan Cubitt
John Cunliffe
Peter Curtis
Tony Curtis
Rachel Cusk
Ivor Cutler
Catherine Czerkawska

David Dabydeen
Fred D'Aguiar
William Dalrymple
Amanda Dalton
Emma Daly
Ita Daly
Wally K. Daly
Sarah Daniels
Margaretta D'Arcy
Charlie Dark
Marjorie Darke
Nick Darke
Julia Darling
Catherine Davidson
Ian Davidson
Amanda Davies
Andrew Davies
Nicola Davies
Ray Davies
Dick Davis
Owen Davis
Susan Davis
Kwame Dawes
Jennifer Dawson
Jill Dawson
Roger Deakin

April de Angelis
Nick Dear
Meaghan Delahunt
Frank Delaney
Chris Dennis
Bob Devereux
Anne Devlin
Polly Devlin
Peter Dickinson
Ann Marie Di
   Mambro
Narinder Dhami
Farukh Dhondy
Michael Dibdin
Tom Disch
Nigel Dodd
Paul Dodgson
Berlie Doherty
David Donachie
Michael Donaghy
Julia Donaldson
Emma Donoghue
Maura Dooley
Tim Dooley
Paul Dornan
Mark Dornford-May
Dianne Doubtfire
Louise Doughty
Fred Downie
John Downie
Terry Downie
Malachy Doyle
Margaret Drabble
Richard Drain
Nick Drake
Robert Drake
C.J. Driver
Jessica Dromcoole
Alan Drury
Carol Ann Duffy
Clare Duffy
Maureen Duffy
Stella Duffy
Ian Duhig
Sarah Dunant
Glen Duncan

Ronald Duncan
Patricia Duncker
Helen Dunmore
Anthony Dunn
Douglas Dunn
Nell Dunn
Paul Dunn
Suzannah Dunn
Frank Dunne
Jane Duran
Paul Durcan
G.F. Dutton
Ilan Dwek
Geoff Dyer
Kutaki Kushari Dyson

Jean Earle
Michael Earley
Amanda Eason
Daniel Easterman
David Edgar
Susan Elderkin
Menna Elfyn
Patricia Elliott
Steve Ellis
Lucy Ellman
Margaret
  Elphingstone
Billie Eltringham
Ruth Elwin Harris
Buchi Emecheta
Lucy English
Anne Enright
Loris Essary
Tony Etchells
Paul Evans
Bernadine Evaristo
Gavin Ewart
Heather Eyles

Ruth Fainlight
Zoe Fairbairns
John Fairfax
Colin Falck
Agneta Falk
U.A. Fanthorpe

Paul Farley
Penelope Farmer
Sebastian Faulks
John Fawcett Wilson
Vicki Feaver
Elaine Feinstein
Alison Fell
Graham Fellowes
James Fenton
Gillian Ferguson
Michael Ffinch
Katie Fforde
Eva Figes
Peter Finch
Gervaise Finn
Tim Firth
Tibor Fischer
Laura Fish
Allen Fisher
Catherine Fisher
Nick Fisher
Roy Fisher
Georgia Fitch
Penelope Fitzgerald
Peter Flannery
Mary Flanagan
Helen Flint
David Flusfeder
Tony Flynn
Peter Forbes
Nigel Forde
John Foster
Roy Foster
Tim Fountain
Catherine Fox
John Fox
Linda France
Miranda France
Matthew Francis
Richard Francis
Donna Francischild
Katherine Frank
Sophie Frank
Gilly Fraser
Paul Fraser
Maureen Freely

Patrick French
James Friel
Tina Fulker
Janice Fuller
John Fuller
Andrew Fusek Peters

Hayden Gabriel
Patrick Gale
Ellen Galford
Janice Galloway
Patrick Galvin
Lucy Gannon
Leon Garfield
Roger Garfitt
Tim Garland
Alan Garner
Elizabeth Garrett
David Gascoyne
William Gaskill
Jonathan Gathorne-
  Hardy
Robert Gathorne-
  Hardy
Jamila Gavin
Jackie Gay
Mike Gayle
Gabriel Gbadamosi
Carlo Gebler
Maggie Gee
Shirley Gee
Jonathan Gems
Pam Gams
Adele Geras
Alan Gibbons
Charles Gibbs
Angie Gilligan
Pamela Gillilan
Jacky Gillott
John Gilmore
Michael Ginsberg
Robert Gittings
Chrissie Gittins
Lesley Glaister
David Glass
John Glenday

Victoria Glendinning
Jon Glover
Martin Glynn
Dennis Goacher
Paul Godfrey
Sheila Goff
William Golding
Stuart Golland
Steve Gooch
Oleg Gordievsky
Giles Gordon
John Gordon
Stewart Gordon
Don Gould
Mick Gowar
Desmond Graham
Margaret Graham
Matthew Graham
W S Graham
Gawn Grainger
Maurice Gran
Cy Grant
Linda Grant
Lesley Grant-Adamson
Alasdair Gray
Ann Gray
Nigel Gray
Sarah Grazebrook
Terry Greaves
Lily Greenham
Stephen Greenhorn
Colin Greenland
Lavinia Greenlaw
Andrew Greig
Noel Greig
John Gribbin
Evgeny Gridneff
Bill Griffiths
Diana Griffiths
Gayle Griffiths
Hannah Griffiths
Steve Griffiths
Philip Gross
David Grubb
Fred Grubb
Harry Guest

Tim Guest
Romesh Gunesekera
Kirsty Gunn
Anil Gupta
Tanika Gupta
Abdulrazak Gurnah
Peter Gutteridge

Helon Habila
Mark Haddon
Tess Hadley
Albyn Hall
Lee Hall
Rebecca Hall
Alyson Hallett
David Halliwell
Grace Hallworth
Michael Hamburger
Rob Hamburger
Alex Hamilton
Hugo Hamilton
Ian Hamilton
Georgina Hammick
Christopher Hampton
Nathalie Handal
Nick Hanna
Sophie Hannah
Johnny Handle
Gillian Hanscombe
Charlie Harcourt
John Harding
Patrick Harkens
Adrian Harman
James Harpur
Anne Harries
Elizabeth Harris
Joanne Harris
Mike Harris
Steve Harris
Wilson Harris
Zinnie Harris
Carey Harrison
M John Harrison
Phil Harrison
Tony Harrison
David Harsent

David Hart
Michael Hartland
John Hartley Williams
Andrew Harvey
John Harvey
Lee Harwood
Geoff Hattersley
Anne Haverty
Chris Hawes
Jim Hawkins
Sarah-Louise Hawkins
Karen Hayes
Carole Hayman
Sian Hayton
Seamus Heaney
Mairi Hedderwick
Iain Heggie
John Hegley
Diane Hendry
Adrian Henri
Philip Hensher
W.N. Herbert
Tracey Herd
Phoebe Hesketh
Theresa Heskins
Kathryn Heyman
Sally Hibbins
Katie Hickman
Professor David Hicks
Nicholas Hicks-Beach
Norman Hidden
Rita Ann Higgins
Roger Highfield
David Hill
Geoffrey Hill
Jim Hill
Justin Hill
Reginald Hill
Selima Hill
Tobias Hill
Danny Hiller
Katie Himms
Thomas Hinde
Barry Hines
Laura Hird
Jack Hirschman

Jim Hitchmough
Russell Hoban
Jo Hodges
Eva Hoffman
Michael Hofmann
Desmond Hogan
Susan Hogg
David Holbrook
Ursula Holden
Dave Holman
Robert Holman
Jane Holland
Tony Holland
Geoffrey Holloway
Alan Hollinghurst
Michael Holroyd
Geraldine Hold
Miroslav Holub
Jeremy Hooker
Adam Hopkins
Sarah Hopkins
Anthony Horovitz
Frances Horovitz
Michael Horovitz
Debbie Horsfield
Kate Horsley
Libby Houston
Elizabeth Jane
  Howard
Kay Howard
Lesley Howarth
Edward Hower
Janni Howker
Trevor Hoyle
Sue Hubbard
Margaret Huber
Louise Hudson
David Huggins
David Hughes
Glyn Hughes
Kathryn Hughes
Ted Hughes
Lucy Hughes-Hallett
Michael Husle
William Humble
Albert Hunt

Martha Hunt
David Hunter
Iain Hunter
Neil Hunter
Susi Hush
Pat Hutchins
Laurence Hutchins
Daniel Huws
Jill Hyem
Paul Hyland

Mark Illis
Mick Imlah
Grace Ingoldby
Kazuo Ishiguro
Debbie Isitt

Kathleen Jamie
Alan Jackson
Leigh Jackson
Mick Jackson
Andrzei Jackowski
Nicki Jackowski
Steve Jacobi
Saul Jaffe
Linda James
P.D. James
Sian James
Robert Adam
  Jamieson
Peter Jay
Stephen Jeffreys
Ray Jenkin
Alan Jenkins
Amy Jenkins
Robin Jenkins
Martin Jenkins
Elizabeth Jennings
Liz Jensen
Amryl Johnson
Jane Johnson
Judith Johnson
Pamela Johnson
Jennifer Johnston
Paul Johnston
Chris Johnstone

Robert Johnstone
Charlotte Jones
Gwyneth Jones
Julia Jones
Mervyn Jones
Neil Jones
Philip Jones Griffiths
Alison Joseph
Jenny Joseph
Gabriel Josipovici
Graham Joyce
John Junkin

Peter Kalu
Sylvia Kantaris
P.J. Kavanagh
Francesca Kay
Jackie Kay
Geraldine Kaye
Liselle Kayla
Judith Kazantzis
H.R.F. Keating
Charlotte Keatley
Richard Kell
Brigit Pegeen Kelly
James Kelman
G. Kelsey
Gene Kemp
George Kendrick
Brendan Kennelly
A.L. Kennedy
Douglas Kennedy
Troy Kennedy Martin
Mel Kenyon
Mimi Khalvati
Thomas Kilroy
Gary Kilworth
Christopher King
Francis King
Phyllis April King
Mark Kingwell
John Kinsella
James Kirkup
Paddy Kitchen
August Kleinzahler
Alanna Knight

Stephen Knight
Steve Knightley
John Knowler
Marius Kociejowski
Tessa Krailing
Lotte Kramer
Hanif Kureishi
Terry Kyan

Aileen La Tourette
Bruce Lacey
R.M. Lamming
John Lane
Reuben Lane
Christine Langan
Brigid Larmour
James Lasdun
Jennifer Lash
Michael Laskey
Jacek Laskowski
John Latham
Tarig Latif
Janet Laurence
Bryony Lavery
Michael Lawrence
Keith Lawley
Bob Lawson
Geoff Lawson
Keith Lawson
Mark Lawson
Hermione Lee
Nicola Le Fanu
Sarah Le Fanu
Gordon Legge
Mike Leggett
Mike Leigh
Alison Leonard
Tom Leonard
Laurence Lerner
Norman Levine
Andrea Levy
Deborah Levy
Brian Lewis
Gwyneth Lewis
Tang Lin
Grevel Lindop

Fredric Lindsay
Toby Litt
Adam Liveley
Penelope Lively
Emmanuel Litvinoff
Henry Livings
Dinah Livingstone
Hilary Llewellyn-
  Williams
Claudia Lloyd
Rick Lloyd
Liz Lochhead
David Lodge
Christopher Logue
Marion Lomax
James Long
Michael Longley
John Lord
Stephen Lowe
Rupert Loydell
Roddy Lumsden
Alison Lurie
Gavin Lyall
Alexis Lykiard
Martin Lynch
Thomas Lynch
Gary Lyons
John Lyons

George MacBeth
Colin MacDonald
Gerard MacDonald
Sharman MacDonald
Carl MacDougall
Barbara Machin
Shena Mackay
Laura Mackie
Bernard MacLaverty
Rory MacLean
Ken MacLeod
Sheila MacLeod
Shaun MacLoughlin
Aonghas MacNeacail
Kevin MacNeil
Catherine MacPhail
Julia MacRae

Barry MacSweeney
Deirdre Madden
Eric Maddern
Wes Magee
Michele Magorian
Paul Magrs
Sarah Maguire
Mary Maher
Derek Mahon
Sara Maitland
Adbul Malik
Anjum Malik
Gerald Mangan
Olivia Manning
Hilary Mantel
Caeia March
Tony Marchant
Jan Mark
E.A. Markham
Lawrence Marks
Adam Mars Jones
Philip Marsden
Henry Marsh
Kevin Marston
Andrew Martin
Cheryl Martin
Christopher Martin
Gillian Martin
Rhona Martin
Anita Mason
Barry Mason
Harold Massingham
Roland Mathias
Sue Matthias
Kath Mattock
Ernest Maxim
Glyn Maxwell
Sarah Maxwell
Kara May
Steve May
Gerda Mayer
Martin Mayes
James Mayhew
Paul Mayhew-Archer
Angela McAllister
Brian McCabe

Patrick McCabe
Bridget McCann
Colum McCann
Thomas McCarthy
Rhys McConnachie
Bill McCormack
Cameron McCracken
Moy McCrory
Robert McCrum
Don McCullin
Alan McDonald
Val McDermid
Tom McGrath
Ian McEwan
John McGahern
Roger McGough
Jimmy McGovern
John McGrath
Medbh McGuckian
Tony McHale
Vincent McInerney
Jamie McKendrick
Duncan McLean
Ian McMillan
Eoin McNamee
Frances McNeil
Jean McNeil
David McNiven
Geoff McQueen
Candia McWilliam
Daniel Meadows
Rebecca Meitlis
Kay Mellor
James Melville
Pauline Melville
Charlotte Mendelson
Chris Meredith
Catherine Merriman
Stanley Middleton
Gavin Millar
Andrew Miller
Brian Miller
Miranda Miller
Patricia Miller
Paul Miller
Roland Miller

Mil Millington
John Milne
Paula Milne
Denise Mina
Anthony Minghella
Robert Minhinnick
Adrian Mitchell
Elma Mitchell
Timothy Mo
John Moat
Deborah Moggach
John Mole
Stephen Mollett
Frances Molloy
Bel Mooney
Hubert Moore
Caroline Moorehead
Cole Moreton
Abi Morgan
Edwin Morgan
Elizabeth Morgan
Esther Morgan
Pete Morgan
Carole Morin
Harold Morland
David Morley
Michael Morpurgo
Tom Morris
Bill Morrison
Blake Morrison
Crysse Morrison
Graham Mort
Penelope Mortimer
Peter Mortimer
Nicholas Mosley
Andrew Motion
Eric Mottram
Abigail Mozley
Robin Mukerjee
Paul Muldoon
Dominic Muldowney
Stephen Mulrine
Rona Munro
Michael Murphy
Sheila Murphy
John Murray

Lavinia Murray
Susan Musgrave
Jonathan Myerson

Beverley Naidoo
Suniti Namjoshi
Marion Nancarrow
Tanya Nash
Hattie Naylor
Patrick Neate
Jan Needles
Denise Neuhaus
Jill Neville
Linda Newbery
Courttia Newland
G.F. Newman
Jenny Newman
Kim Newman
Lauretta Ngcobo
William Nicholson
Charles Nicholl
Grace Nichols
Norman Nicholson
Eileen Ni Chuilleanain
Nuala Ni Dhomhnaill
Chris Niel
Dorothy Nimmo
David Nobbs
Andy Noble
Carol Noble
Leslie Norris
Elizabeth North
Mick North
Sam North
Jeff Nuttall
Simon Nye

Meredith Oakes
Philip Oakes
Sean O'Brien
Eoin O'Callaghan
Chris O'Connell
Bridget O'Connor
Bernard O'Donoghue
Maggie O'Farrell
Tamsin Oglesby

Timothy O'Grady
Andrew O'Hagan
Sean O'Huigan
Rebecca O'Rourke
Ben Okri
June Oldham
Jon Oram
John Ormond
Will Osborne
Maggie O'Sullivan
Alice Oswald
Nick Otty
Caroline Oulton
Agnes Owen
Gareth Owen
Olusola Oyeleye

Ruth Padel
Kathy Page
Louise Page
Charles Palliser
William Palmer
Eric Plaice
Tom Paine
Phil Parker
Dean Parkin
Suzan-Lori Parks
Martin Parr
Don Paterson
Jill Paton Walsh
Kay Patrick
Brian Patten
Glenn Patterson
Piers Paul Read
Tom Paulin
Andrew Payne
John Peacock
Meg Peacocke
Philippa Pearce
Iain Pears
Tim Pears
Geoff Pearson
Bob Pegg
Chris Penfold
Tina Pepler
Emily Perkins

Nigel Perkins
Wendy Perriam
Alan Perry
Mario Petrucci
Brian Phelan
Gilbert Phelps
Caryl Phillips
Mike Phillips
Justine Picardie
Tom Pickard
Katherine Pierpoint
Geraldine Pilgrim
Christopher Pilling
Darryl Pinckney
Winsome Pinnock
David Pirie
Jill Pirrie
Anne Pivcevic
Davie Plante
Peter Plate
Alan Plater
Barney Platts-Mills
Piers Plowright
Patricia Pogson
Devorah Pope
Peter Porter
Phil Porter
Tim Porter
Jem Poster
Jennifer Potter
Joan Poulson
Tom Pow
Neil Powell
Patricia Powell
M.S. Power
David Pownall
Mary Prestige
Trevor Preston
Anthony Price
Christopher Priest
Alison Prince
Gwyn Pritchard
David Profumo
Sheenagh Pugh
Kate Pullinger
Philip Pullman

Rob Pursey
Rodney Pybus
Michael Pye

Eileen Quinn

Lisanne Radice
Simon Rae
Craig Raine
Kathleen Raine
Deborah Randall
Elain Randell
Ravinder Randhawa
Ian Rankin
Jennifer Rankin
Peter Ransley
Ian Rashid
Mark Ravenhill
Martin Ravenhill
Graham Rawle
Jeff Rawle
Tom Rawling
Tom Raworth
Mary Rayner
Richard Rayner
Peter Reading
Chris Reason
Peter Redgrove
Jeremy Reed
David Rees
Deryn Rees-Jones
Christopher Reid
Christine Reid
Neil Rennie
Nick Revell
Alastair Reynolds
Oliver Reynolds
David Richard Fox
Ben Richards
Vanessa Richards
Harry Ritchie
Graham Rigby
Joan Riley
Maurice Riordan
Harry Ritchie
Rob Ritchie

Adam Roberts
Andy Roberts
Joe Roberts
Katherine Roberts
Michèle Roberts
Sue Roberts
Susan Roberts
Robin Robertson
Stanley Robertson
Philip Robinson
Roger Robinson
Rony Robinson
Tom Robinson
Justina Robson
Paul Roche
Frank Rodger
Christian Rodska
Susan Roe
Jane Rogers
Laura Rogers White
Neil Rollinson
Jon Ronson
James Roose-Evans
Dilys Rose
Tony Rose
Michael Rosen
Jack Rosenthal
Bess Ross
Jacob Ross
Leone Ross
Leon Rosselson
Anne Rouse
John Row
Peter Rowe
John Rowe Townsend
Kate Rowland
Nicholas Royle
Bernice Rubens
Anthony Rudolph
Carol Rumens
Christopher Rush
Salman Rushdie
Kay Russell
Mary Russell
Willy Russell
Julie Rutterford

John Ryle
Margaret Ryan
Tracy Ryan
Geoff Ryman

Allen Saddler
Sapphire
Lawrence Sail
Eva Salzman
Jacob Sam-La Rose
Anthony Sampson
Ann Sansom
Peter Sansom
Diederick Santer
Tim Satchell
Carole Satyamurti
Paul Sayer
Josephine Saxton
Justin Sbresni
Michelle Scally
William Scammell
Vernon Scannell
Lucy Scher
Michael Schmidt
Myra Schneider
John Scotney
Hugh Scott
Lawrence Scott
Mary Scott
Peter Scupham
Jeremy Seal
Will Self
Sam Selvon
Sudeep Sen
Olive Senior
Howard Sergeant
Kadija Sessay
Angela Sewell
John Sewell
Miranda Seymour
Nicolas Shakespeare
Kamilla Shamsie
Jo Shapcott
Trevor Sharpe
Dick Sharples
Clare Shaw

Robert Shaw
Dave Sheasby
Owen Sheers
Dyan Sheldon
Jeremy Sheldon
Yvonne Shelton
Mike Shepherd
Nona Shepphard
Robert Sheppard
Alan Sheridan
Tessa Sheridan
Dave Shewell
Lionel Shriver
Henry Shukman
Penelope Shuttle
Labi Siffre
Shelly Silas
Melanie Silgardo
Jon Silkin
Alan Sillitoe
Pat Silva Laskey
James Simmons
John Simmons
Barry Simner
Dave Simpson
Helen Simpson
Matt Simpson
Clive Sinclair
Iain Sinclair
Lemn Sissay
C.H. Sisson
Charlie Skelton
John Sladek
Guy Slater
Gillian Slovo
Dorothea Smartt
A.C.H. Smith
Ali Smith
Anthony Smith
Caroline E. Smith
Emma Smith
Joan Smith
John Smith
Ken Smith
Martin Smith
Paul Smith

Romy Smith
Sid Smith
Zadie Smith
Ade Solanke
Mahendra Solanki
Piotr Sommer
Ahdaf Soueif
Tim Souster
Frances Spalding
Tom Spanbauer
Alan Spence
Peter Spence
Colin Spencer
David Spenser
Anne Spillard
Duncan Sprott
Lisa St Aubin de Teran
Pauline Stainer
Jon Stallworthy
John Stammers
Michael Standen
Martin Stannard
Liz Steele
Roger Stennett
Jaci Stephen
Jenny Stephens
Heidi Stephenson
Shelagh Stephenson
Anne Stevenson
Bruce Stewart
Margaret Stewart
Sue Stewart
Nick Stimson
Hugh Stoddart
Martin Stokes
Julia Stoneham
Edward Storey
Jack Trevor Story
Peter Straughan
Nell Stroud
Alexander Stuart
Chris Stuart
Alicia Stubbersfield
Jean Stubbs
Paul Stubbs
Tristam Sturrock

David Sulkin
Henry Sutton
Bob Swash
Matthew Sweeney
Amanda Swift
Graham Swift
Robert Swindells
Meera Syal
Ruth Symes
Julian Symons
Michael Symmons-
 Roberts
George Szirtes

Kim Taplin
George Tardios
Steve Tasane
Cyril Tawney
Andrew Taylor
Cheryl Taylor
D.J. Taylor
John Taylor
Susan Taylor
Sue Teddern
Emma Tennant
Peter Terson
D.M. Thomas
Ifor Thomas
Sue Thomas
Alice Thomas Ellis
Alice Thompson
Brian Thompson
David Thompson
Laura Thompson
Adam Thorpe
Chris Thorpe
Ann Thwaite
Anthony Thwaite
Colin Thubron
Lawrence Till
Peter Tinniswood
Nick Toczek
Susan Todd
Colm Toibin
Maria Tolly
Barry Took

Sue Townshend
Lorna Tracy
Barbara Trapido
Joanna Traynor
Rose Tremain
Lynn Truss
Eva Tucker
Gael Turnbull
Bill Turner
John Turner
Peter Turner 'Peanuts'
Lisa Tuttle

Jenny Uglow
Barry Unsworth

Ardashir Vakir
Parminder Vir
Clara Villiamy

David Wade
John Wain
Jeff Wainwright
Stephen Wakelam
Christopher Wakling
Anne Waldman
Glen Walford
Nick Walker
Ted Walker
John Walsh
Michelene Wandor
Nick Warburton
Marina Warner
Jean Warr
Tony Warren
Gregory Warren
 Wilson
Julie Wassmer
Carran Waterfield
James Watson
Williams Watson
Auberon Waugh
Nick Webb
Derek Weeks
Judy Weeks
Arabella Weir

Doffy Weir
Judith Weir
Daniel Weissbort
Fay Weldon
Dee Wells
Marion Wells
Nigel Wells
Robert Wells
Irvine Welsh
Louise Welsh
Louise Wener
Timberlake Werten-
  baker
Arnold Wesker
Mary Wesley
Robert Westall
Alex Wheatle
Sara Wheeler
Christopher Wicking
Edmund White
Phil Whitaker
Helen Whitehead
Liz Whitelaw
E.A. Whithead
John Whitworth
Christopher Whyte
Susan Wicks
Peter Wiegold
Marianne Wiggins
Ella Wildridge
Pier Wilkie
Margaret Wilkinson
Colin Will
C.K. Williams
Chris Williams
Edward Williams
Heathcote Williams
Hugo Williams
John Williams
Roy Williams
Simon Williams
Sioned Williams
Malcolm Williamson
Diz Willis
Emily Wills
J.C. Wilsher

Anthony Wilson
Colin Wilson
Gina Wilson
Hamish Wilson
Kate Wilson
Laura Wilson
Leslie Wilson
Snoo Wilson
Sue Wilson
Elisabeth Winkler
Terri Windling
Valerie Windsor
Pat Winslow
Angus Wolfe-Murray
Chris Wood
Jim Woodland
Gerard Woodward
Will Woodward
Henry Woolf
Sophie Woolley
Sally Worboyes
David Wright
Kit Wright
Olwen Wymark
June Wyndham
  Davies
Diana Wynne-Jones

Cliff Yates
Sheila Yeger
Louisa Young
Gary Younge

Theatre
The Clod Ensemble
I.O.U. Theatre

APPENDIX 3:
SPONSORS, FUNDERS
AND BENEFACTORS

Support for its administration and for the Centre Directors' salaries at the Hurst:
The Barnes Fairbairn Foundation

Donations to its Bursary Endowment Fund:
The Arts Foundation
Pat Barker
Roy Blackman
C.T. Bowring and Company Ltd
Mavis Carter
The David Cohen Family
    Charitable Trust
The John S. Cohen Foundation
The Cornwall Charitable Trust
The Dulverton Trust
The Ronald Duncan Foundation
Duncan Lawrie Ltd, Private Bankers
Mrs T.S. Eliot
The Elmgrant Trust
Faber & Faber Ltd
The Fishmongers' Company
The Friends of the Arvon
    Foundation (for the David
    Pease Bursary)
Cohn and Anna Frizzell Charitable
    Trust
The Golden Bottle Trust
The Gregg Charitable Trust
The Worshipful Company of
    Grocers
The Haberdashers' Company
The Halifax Building Society
Josephine Hart
Susan Hill
Hillsdown Holdings plc
The E.S. Hogg Charitable Trust

The Frances Horovitz Memorial Fund
Hal Hudson
David Hunter
P.D. James
The Allen Lane Foundation
John Lewis Partnership plc
Lloyds Bank plc
Longman Group UK Ltd
Macmillan Publishers Ltd
Marks & Spencer plc
The Marsh Christian Trust
The Mercers' Company
John and Antoinette Moat
Jill Molnar
News International plc
Jane Nissen
Portsmouth and Sunderland
    Newspapers
E.L. Rathbone Charitable Trust
The Rank Foundation
The Russell Trust
Transworld Publishers Ltd
Save & Prosper Educational Trust
The Scottish Arts Council
Shell UK Ltd
The Skinners' Company
W H Smith & Son Group
Jacqueline de Sibour
Sotheby's
The M.J.C. Stone Charitable Trust
Sue Teddern
United News & Media pIc
Walker Books Ltd
The Wates Foundation
Whitbread & Company plc
The Martyn Wiley Memorial Fund
The Willison Family (Hilary
    Torrance)

Donations for bursaries:
The Laura Ashley Foundation
The John Ellerman Foundation
The Ernest CookTrust
J. Paul Getty Jr Charitable Trust
The Leverhulme Trust
Jerwood Charitable Foundation

Donations for courses for teachers and teacher trainees:
The Ernest Cook Trust
The Esmee Fairbairn Charitable
   Trust
The Kirby Laing Foundation
News International plc

Donations for schools:
The Ernest Cook Trust
Halifax plc
The Hedley Foundation
Susan Hill
Pearson Television
The Tudor Trust
The Wates Foundation

Donations for the purchase and adaptation of Totleigh Barton:
The Clothworkers' Foundation
The Dulverton Trust
The Foundation for Sport and
   the Arts
The Hedley Foundation
Selima Hill
E.S. Hogg Charitable Trust
John and Antoinette Moat
The Pilgrim Trust
The Rayne Foundation

Donations for young writers' apprenticeships:
Jerwood Charitable Foundation

Donations of £250 or more for the restoration of the Bee Bole Wall at Lumb Bank:
Abbey National Charitable Trust

The Chase Charity
The Friends of Arvon
Mrs T.S. Eliot
Andrew Kerr-Garrett
A.E. Pease

And from the many individuals who have sponsored a stone, or made smaller donations.

Donations for the purchase and adaptation of the Hurst:
The Clothworkers' Foundation
The J. Paul Getty Jr Charitable
   Trust
The Foyle Foundation
Karen Grieve
Anthony Howard
The Kirby Laing Foundation
The Millichope Foundation
Helen Osborne
The Rayne Foundation
The Bernard Sunley Charitable
   Foundation
Garfield Weston Foundation
Viscount Windsor
The Po-Shing Woo Charitable
   Foundation

Two donations towards information technology and a course for science writers:
The Royal Commission for the
   Exhibition of 1851

Donations to the Centres:
The Friends of the Arvon
   Foundation

Sponsorship of funding events and publications:
A.D.M. Investor Services
BAT
The Classic Drinks Company Ltd
The *Daily Telegraph*

Philippe Foriel Destezet
Duncan Lawrie Ltd, Private
  Bankers
Mrs T.S. Eliot
Enterprise Oil plc
Faber & Faber Ltd
The Robert Gavron Charitable
  Trust
Hodder Headline Ltd
The Jerwood Charitable
  Foundation
Laing & Cruickshank Investment
  Management Ltd
The Levy Foundation
Media Fund
Merchant Group
Rodenstock (UK) Ltd
Scottish Equitable plc
The Bernard Sunley Charitable
  Foundation
The Rutland Trust

Undesignated donations:
Andersen Press
A.W.G. Literary Agency
Rupert Beeley
Celia Brayfield
John Brown Publishing
P.H.G. Cadbury Charitable Trust
Thomas Sivewright Catto
  Charitable Settlement
Centrica plc
The Cluff Foundation
The Courage Charitable Trust
Coutts Bank
Leopold de Rothschild
Deutsche Morgan Grenfell
  Group plc
Ethical Investors Group
Amanda and Toby Faber
Farrer & Co. Charitable Trust
Foreign & Colonial Management
  Ltd
Mr & Mrs C. Formby
Garfield Weston Foundation
Michael J. Gee

Gidleigh Park
The Golden Bottle Trust
Joanna Goodwin
The Mabel Green Trust
Lord Griffiths
The Worshipful Company of
  Grocers
Thom Gunn
A.M. Heath
J.G. Hogg Charitable Trust
S.M. Charitable Trust
The Estate of Madeline Dorothy
  Mayne
Peters Fraser & Dunlop
Mark Le Fanu
Charles Nettleford
James St Aubyn
Mary Sheepshanks
South Square Trust
The Westminster Foundation
Susan Wicks
The Rt Hon Lord Younger

And support from many individuals, in particular those who have
visited its Centres.

**Moniack Mhor acknowledges the
loan of books:**
The Scottish Poetry Library

APPENDIX 4:
KEY DATES FOR ARVON

1968	First course, at the Beaford Centre
1969	First Arts Council of England grant
1972	First course at Totleigh Barton
1972	The Arvon Foundation Ltd incorporated
1973	The Arvon Foundation registered as a Charity
1973	Sir Havelock Hudson Chairman
1974	David Pease National Director
1975	First course at Lumb Bank
1976	Friends of Arvon inaugural meeting
1980	First Arvon Foundation International Poetry Competition
1986	Carol Hughes Chairman
1989	Arvon acquires Lumb Bank after national fundraising campaign
1991	Lawrence Sail Chairman
1993	First course at Moniack Mhor
1994	Professor Brian Cox Chairman
1996	Arvon acquires Totleigh Barton with Arts Council Capital Lottery grant
1997	Sir Robin Chichester-Clark Chairman
1999	Arvon's London office opens
1999	Arvon acquires The Hurst with Arts Council Capital Lottery grant
2000	Moniack Mhor operating independently, funded by Moniack Trust and Scottish Arts Council
2001	Helen Chaloner National Director
2001	Prudence Skene Chairman
2003	First course at The Hurst
2003	Stephanie Anderson National Director

INDEX